# Koi

**An Owner's Guide To**

**A HAPPY HEALTHY FISH**

Howell Book House

**Howell Book House**
An Imprint of Macmillan General Reference USA
A Pearson Education Macmillan Company
1633 Broadway
New York, NY 10019

Library of Congress Cataloging-in-Publication Data
Skomal, Gregory.
     Koi : an owner's guide to a happy healthy fish / [Gregory Skomal].
        p. cm.
     Includes bibliographical references.
     ISBN 1-58245-032-3

     1. Koi.     I. Title.
SF458.K64S56     1999
639.3'7f483—dc21                98-51715
                                    CIP

Manufactured in the United States of America
10 9 8 7 6 5 4 3 2 1
Series Director: Amanda Pisani
Series Assistant Director: Michele Matrisciani
Book Design: Michele Laseau
Cover Design: Iris Jeromnimon
Illustration: Casey Price, Laura Robbins, and Brian Towse
Photography:
  *Front cover by Tom Graham*
  *Inset Courtesy of* KOI USA
  Laurie Connable: 43, 45, 46, 47, 48, 68, 97
  Tom Graham: ii, 5, 10, 11, 15, 17, 18 (top), 19 (top), 20, 21, 23 (top), 25, 30, 32–33,
  71, 76–77, 78, 89, 94, 99, 102, 106, 112, 115, 118
  KOI USA: 2–3, 16, 24, 27, 31, 104
Production Team: Carrie Allen, Toi Davis, Clint Lahnen, Heather Pope, Carol
  Sheehan, Dennis Sheehan, and Terri Sheehan

# Contents

# The
# Joy

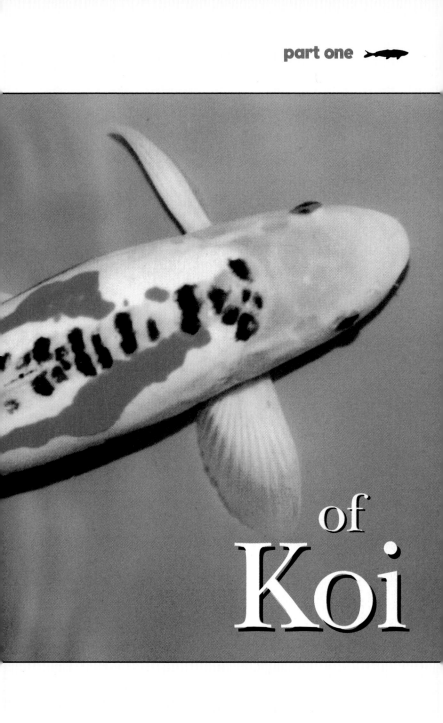

of
Koi

# External Features of Koi

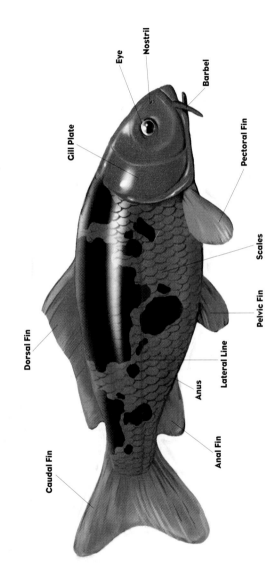

Eye

Nostril

Barbel

Gill Plate

Pectoral Fin

Dorsal Fin

Scales

Pelvic Fin

Anus

Lateral Line

Caudal Fin

Anal Fin

# What
## Are Koi ?

Considered by many to be the most elegant and colorful of the freshwater fishes, koi have become popular inhabitants of domestic garden ponds. The large size and space require-ments of koi preclude their inclusion in the average fresh-water aquarium. Therefore, if you want to keep koi, plan on establishing an ornamental or garden pond in an area where you will be able to fully enjoy and maintain your pet koi. This book will provide you with the basics of establishing a pond, properly stocking it with koi, and maintaining, feeding and breeding healthy and attractive fish. But before we move into these areas, let's first estab-

lish exactly what koi are, their origin, morphology and biology.

5

Koi (which is an adaptation of the formal Japanese name of *nishikigoi*) are actually just colorful mutations of the common carp, *Cyprinus carpio*. These carp mutations were first recorded in Persia and China around 2,500 years ago. The Chinese raised carp for food, a practice that was adopted by Japanese rice farmers. Many feel that it was these Japanese farmers of the Niigata Prefecture who noticed colored mutants among the normally drab gray carp. By meticulously selecting these fish and breeding them over many generations, a number of koi varieties were established at that time. Surprisingly, until the twentieth century, koi were only known among these farmers of the Niigata region of Japan. This changed dramatically in the early part of the century when several varieties were exhibited at a Tokyo exhibition. The popularity of this fish rapidly expanded throughout the country and eventually to other parts of the world. Today, koi are bred in North America, western Europe, Israel and Singapore, but the Japanese remain the primary breeders of the world's finest koi varieties.

## THE CYPRINID FAMILY

Koi are one of the 2,000 species of fish that make up the cyprinid family of fish. Many cyprinids are popular fish for the home aquarium, such as the Clown Loach, the Tiger Barb, the Zebra Fish and the Red-Tailed Rasbora. With so many different species, there are obviously many differences between the members of this fish family. One behavior that all cyprinids share is their method of reproduction—cyprinids lay eggs that are then fertilized outside of their body.

Koi belong to the largest family of fishes known as the Cyprinidae, which contains over 2,000 species. The cyprinids have the widest continuous distribution of any freshwater fish family. They are very hardy fish and can generally exist in a wide variety of conditions ranging from quiet vegetated ponds to silty, turbid rivers. They are also capable of tolerating wide temperature fluctuations. A close relative of the koi is another common aquarium inhabitant, the goldfish, *Carassius auratus*. While koi and goldfish share many common characteristics, koi attain larger sizes and can be readily differentiated from goldfish by the presence of small whiskers or barbels on either side of their mouth.

Although selective breeding has produced a very wide range of morphological varieties of koi, all koi are scientifically classified as a single species, *Cyprinus carpio*. As a species, all koi possess the same basic external and internal features and general anatomy. They are a fast-growing, large species of fish reaching 7 inches in length at 1 year, 12 inches at 2 years and 16 inches or more at 3 years. Koi can grow as large as 36 inches and weigh over forty-five pounds, but more typically reach 20 to 22 inches in the average ornamental pond. Life expectancy in good environmental conditions can be as long as 50 to 70 years.

## Body Form

Koi typically have a rounded body that is fusiform in shape, thickest in the middle and tapered at either end. The body shape of koi makes them excellent swimmers that are capable of fast bursts of speed when they are threatened. However, koi generally swim lazily through the water with an easy-going style.

## Fins

Almost all species of fish have fins in one form or another. The fins are critically important appendages that allow the fish to propel, stabilize, maneuver and stop. In some cases, fins have developed to protect the fish as well. Again, depending on the type of fish and the habitat it lives in, the fins can take on many shapes and functions.

Koi possess fins that are both medial (unpaired) and lateral (paired).

*Koi have a rounded body that is thickest in the middle and tapered at either end. Even though they look a bit like torpedoes, koi tend to swim rather leisurely.*

The pectoral fins are the forward-most paired fins. These fins act to help the koi stabilize, turn, rotate, maneuver, hover and swim backward. The pectoral fins are found just behind and below the gills on each side of the fish, under the midline of the body. The pectoral fins are also used to fan the substrate when the fish is foraging for food. The pelvic or ventral fins are also paired and are located on the underside of the fish at the mid-body. In general, the pelvic fins are used for directional changes and enable the fish to move up and down in the water. The single unpaired dorsal fin is located on the top of the koi. This fin is used to stabilize the fish, keeping it upright in the water. The dorsal fin can be lowered to reduce drag during rapid

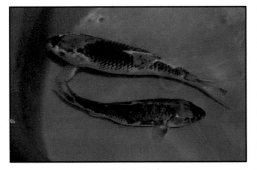

swimming. The anal fin is also unpaired. This fin is located on the underside of the fish, close to the tail behind the anal opening. Like the dorsal fin, the anal fin is used to stabilize the fish during swimming. The caudal or tail fin is an unpaired fin which is largely responsible for propelling the koi forward. This fin is the source of forward momentum for the fish and can also assist in turning and braking. The forked shape of the koi's tail is indicative of the speed that these fish are capable of attaining.

*Koi derive their lovely colors from pigment cells in their skin. The scales are actually translucent and colorless.*

## Scales

The bodies of koi are typically covered with a large number of small scales, although some varieties have fewer, large scales or no scales at all. The scales are composed of a hard, bony substance and serve to protect the fish, reducing the chance of injuries and infection. Covering the scales is a very thin layer of epidermal tissue that contains mucous cells. These cells produce the slimy texture that we normally attribute to fish. The mucous coating on fish not only protects the koi against injury and infection, but helps the fish swim more easily in the water, reducing the friction between the body and the denser water itself. If the mucous layer is damaged, the koi may develop skin problems and secondary infections.

## Skin

The source of the vibrant colors of ornamental koi comes from specialized pigment cells called chromatophore in the dermal layer of the skin. The scales of koi are actually translucent and lack color. The color of the fish depends on the types of chromatophore present. There are generally three types of chromatophore in fish: melanophores, xanthophores and iridophores. Melanophores give fish the darker colors of black, brown and blue; xanthophores produce the colors of red, yellow and orange; and iridophores contain guanine crystals that give the silvery shine common to many koi. Chromatophore are enervated, allowing koi to shift their coloration either lighter or darker. These color changes are generally indicative of stress and should be used to monitor the health of your koi.

## Swim Bladder

Living in the dense medium of water presents a few problems for fish, one of which is buoyancy. Maintaining a certain level in the water column without having to expend a lot of energy is very important to fish. Therefore, most species have special organs called swim bladders, and koi are no exception. This gas-filled sac located in the abdominal cavity near the backbone of the fish acts as a "life vest," keeping the koi at the correct level in the water column. Although there are many types of swim bladders in fish, koi possess a two-chambered type; the forward chamber is partially elastic and can expand, while the rear chamber is inelastic.

> ### SWIM BLADDER BLESSINGS
>
> The remarkable swim bladder not only helps to keep your koi afloat, it also reduces your fish's energy requirements. Fish, such as sharks, that have no swim bladder, must either remain near the bottom or be strong swimmers.

In addition to its role in buoyancy control, the swim bladder also helps to mechanically amplify sound for better hearing in koi.

## Ingestion

The mouth of the koi is typical of most bottom-feeders. That is, it is located below the midline of the head and directed down. The presence of barbels on either side of the mouth further supports the bottom-feeding habit, as these highly specialized sensory organs are used to locate food in the bottom. Despite these anatomical adaptations, domestic koi will rise to the surface to feed in your pond. Like all cyprinids, koi lack teeth in their jaws. Instead, they have paired rows of pharyngeal teeth in the back of their mouth, which are used to crush food.

The digestive system of koi is slightly different from most fish and correlates with their predominantly vegetarian diet. Koi and related cyprinids lack a true stomach, but have long intestinal tracts. This coiled intestine can be up to five times the length of the fish. Ground food passes down the esophagus into the intestine where it is digested by enzymes and other secretions before passing out the anus.

*If you look care-fully, you can see the gill flap on the side of this koi's head.*

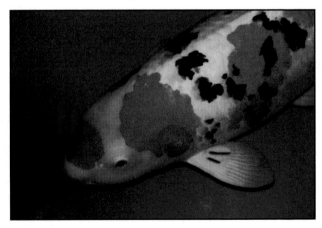

## Respiration

Among the most primary of the basic needs of fish is oxygen. Like land animals, fish are living creatures that require oxygen to live. However, fish must derive oxygen from water and have specialized organs called gills that allow them to do so. The gills of a fish are analogous to our lungs—they provide oxygen to and remove carbon dioxide from the blood of the fish. The oxygen is then transported by the blood to the tissues of the fish where it is utilized to produce energy.

Most fish, including koi, have four gills on each side of the head which are protected by a singular gill flap or operculum. To breathe, water is taken into the mouth by the fish and passed over the gills and out the operculum. As water passes over the membranes and filaments of the gills, oxygen is removed and carbon dioxide is excreted. To accomplish this, the gills have a very high number of blood vessels that deliver the oxygen to the rest of the fish. The gills also function to help maintain water balance in the fish.

## Senses

With few exceptions, koi and other fish have no less than five senses that they use to feed, avoid predators, communicate and reproduce.

### Sight

The eyes of most fishes are similar to our own, except that they lack eyelids and their irises work much slower. The location of the spherical lenses of fish eyes renders most fish nearsighted. The sensitivity of the visual system in koi and its relatives is greatest in the orange spectrum, which matches the wavelength of diffuse light that is present in the murky, shallow, natural aquatic habitats of these fish.

*Like most fish, koi hear sound vibrations passing through the water that reverberate in the fish's inner ear.*

### Hearing

Water is a much more efficient conductor of sound than air is. Therefore, sound carries much farther and faster in water than in air. Most fish do not

possess external ears, but rather an inner ear structure not noticeable on the outside of the fish. The auditory component of the inner ear consists of the sacculus and the lagena, which house the sensory components of hearing, the otoliths. Sound vibrations pass through

11

the water, through the fish's body, and reverberate the otoliths in the inner ear. As with other vertebrates, the inner ear of fish is also important in maintaining equilibrium and balance.

## Smell

Fish have external nasal passages called nares, that allow water to pass into and out of the olfactory organ located above their mouth and below their eyes. Water flows through the nares and into the olfactory pits, where odors are perceived and communicated to the brain via a large nerve. The olfactory system of the fish is not attached to the respiratory system like it is in humans, but remains isolated from the mouth and gills. Smell is particularly important in prey and mate detection in fishes. In koi, the nasal passages are located just forward of the eyes.

## Taste

Taste is generally a close range sense in fishes and is especially helpful in the identification of both food and noxious substances. In addition to being in the mouth, the taste buds of fishes are located on several external surfaces like their skin, lips and fins. In koi, the taste buds are numerous in the mouth cavity, the skin surrounding the mouth and on the tips of the barbels.

### THE LATERAL LINE— A SIXTH SENSE?

A fish's lateral line almost serves as a sixth sense. This very sensitive organ gives a fish up-to-the-minute information on its surroundings. Water vibrations are transmitted through the lateral line to the fish's brain. The lateral line on koi is easily seen along the fish's side.

## Touch

Fish have very specialized organs comprising the lateral line system, which allows them to detect water movements. Sensory receptors lying along the surface of the fish's body in low pits or grooves detect water displacement and therefore give the fish a sensation of touch. The lateral line is easily visible along the sides of koi. This unique system helps the fish to detect other fishes and to avoid obstacles.

# chapter 2

# Varieties
## of
## Koi

As mentioned earlier, a number of morphological varieties of koi have been created over the years. Because many of the koi varieties were established in Japan, Japanese names and terminology are typically used to describe koi. Accordingly, koi terminology can be a bit confusing to the novice koi enthusi-

ast. In addition, differences and difficulties associated with Japanese translations further complicate koi classification. In many cases, koi terminology can differ greatly between sources. In this book, I have tried to present the most traditional classifications of koi. But be aware that other references may use different names for the same fish, or different spellings of the same name. Nonetheless, no koi book would be complete without some discussion of koi varieties.

The important thing to remember is that regardless of the name, your choice of koi as a beginner should be those that please you most. First master the basics of proper care of healthy koi and leave the intricacies of koi classification to the advanced hobbyist.

# How Koi Are Classified

Japanese classification of koi varieties is based on several features including color, patterns and markings, and scale type and arrangement. With reference to coloration, koi will generally bear from one to three body colors, and their Japanese names will reflect this. Typically, those with a single color will be named accordingly, and those with multiple colors generally possess multiple names with the latter name describing the background color on the fish. Descriptive Japanese terms are often used to suggest patterns, color and markings. For example, a *karasu,* which means "crow," is a black koi. Four types of scales are recognized in koi: normal (fully scaled with high metallic sheen), *doitsu* (large sparse scales), leather (lacking scales) and *gin rin* (scales with a dull sheen). Japanese terminology is also used to describe the various types of scales.

The Japanese classification of koi is comprised of thirteen major varieties that are used for judging koi during competitions. There are, however, several types within each variety. All of the major varieties have their own Japanese names, and the types within each variety have names as well. These names range from basic Japanese words for color to names of Japanese emperors who reigned at the time the variety was developed. Readers should consult the glossary in chapter 10 for additional translations of koi-related terminology.

Not all koi fanciers agree about the thirteen recognized varieties of koi, but most students of koi feel they are as follows:

1. *Asagi* and *Shusui.*

2. *Bekko.*

3. *Hikari-moyomono.*

4. *Hikari Utsurimono.*

5. *Kawarimono.*

6. *Kinginrin.*

7. *Kohaku.*

8. *Koromo.*

9. *Ogon.*

10. *Showa Sanshoku* (also known as *Showa Sanke*).

11. *Taisho Sanshoku* (also known as *Taisho Sanke*).

12. *Tancho.*

13. *Utsurimono.*

Because these Japanese words mean little to the novice koi enthusiast, I offer the following brief descriptions of each variety as well as some examples of types within each variety. This should provide the newcomer with the rudimentary means by which to choose, identify, and/or classify his or her koi.

## Asagi and Shusui

Due to their similarity, these two varieties of koi are generally combined for the purposes of competition. *Asagi* were developed over 150 years ago. They are scaled, pale blue koi with orange/red below the lateral line and on the pectoral fins. High-quality *Asagi* must have a uniform blue coloration and the scales have a reticulated (net-like), pinecone pattern on the back.

*Shusui* are *doitsu asagi* with large, dark blue scales along the back and lateral line. You will recall that *doitsu* scales are large and reduced in number.

Asagi *(large fish at bottom),* Shusui *(small fish).*

*Shusui* were bred from the *Asagi* variety and also have a blue back with orange/red below the lateral line and on the pectoral fins.

15

Common examples:

*Hana Shusui,* red markings on both sides of the body and abdomen, extending to the tail.

*Hi Shusui,* red from abdomen to back.

# Bekko

These koi, which were developed in the early 1800s, have characteristic tortoise shell patterns. While many *Bekko* are white, other colors may include red, orange or yellow highlighted with black patches called *sumi.*

*Bekko.*

Common examples:

*Aka Bekko,* red body with *sumi.*

*Ki Bekko,* yellow body with *sumi.*

*Shiro Bekko,* white body with *sumi.*

# Hikari-moyomono

The Japanese name for this variety translates as "metallic pattern." These koi have two colors, and have either a colored pattern over a metallic base or two metallic colors. These bright colors may include platinum white, copper red or jet-black. The head region of these fish is free of markings.

Common examples:

*Hariwake,* orange or gold pattern on platinum body.

*Kikusui,* platinum *doitsu* with yellow waves.

*Kinsui,* metallic red coloration.

*Yamabuki Hariwake,* platinum body with yellow patterns.

*Yamatonishiki,* metallic white with red and black patterns.

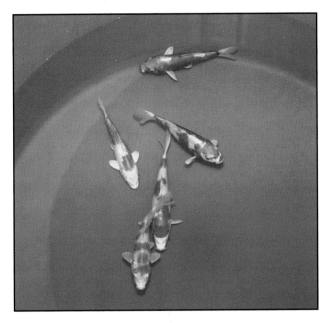

*Hikari-moyomono.*

# Hikari Utsurimono

This variety of koi includes two- and three-colored fish with distinctive metallic scales. High-quality koi of this variety have bright metallic patterns and black markings on the head.

Common examples:

*Gin Showa,* metallic silver body with black and red patterns.

*Kin Hi Utsuri,* black body with golden metallic red pattern.

*Kin Ki Utsuri,* black body with golden metallic yellow pattern.

*Kin Showa,* white body with black and golden metallic red patterns.

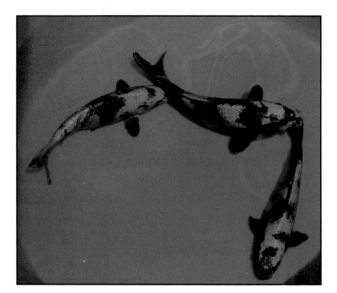

*Hikari
Utsurimono.*

# Kawarimono

Some translate this group as "unusual ones." Generally, this variety includes koi that do not fit into any of the other recognized varieties.

Common examples:

*Goshiki,* five body colors—black with red, white, brown and blue.

*Hajiro,* black body with white tips on fins.

*Karasugoi,* black-colored body.

*Kawarimono.*

*Ki Goi,* yellow body with variable fin colors, standard or *doitsu* scales.

*Kumonryu,* black body with white line on back and sides.

# Kinginrin

This variety of koi has a very bright metallic sheen (the word *"Kinginring"* means golden, silvery scale) that covers the colored patterns underneath. These metallic markings differ in distribution and appearance depending on the type of koi.

Common examples:

*Ginrin,* silver scales on white portions of the body.

*Ginrin Bekko,* silver scales on a white body with black spots.

*Kinginrin Kohaku,* gold and silver markings on a red and white body.

*Kinginrin Sanke,* gold and silver scales on a red, black and white body.

*Kinginrin.*

*Kohaku.*

# Kohaku

The *Kohaku* variety of koi is among the most popular and readily available to the koi enthusiast. *Kohaku* have a white body with red markings. Developed almost 200 years ago, it remains a favorite of the Japanese. *Kohaku* koi may have normal or *doitsu* scales and always lack *sumi* (black markings).

Common examples:

*Aka Muji,* predominantly red *Kohaku.*

*Godan,* five red patterns on body.

*Goten Zakura,* red cherry blossom pattern.

*Inazuma,* lightning-shaped pattern on back.

*Ippon,* one continuous red pattern on body.

*Kuchibeni,* red markings on head and lips.

*Nidan,* two red patterns on body.

*Omoyo,* red wavy pattern on back.

*Sandan,* three red patterns on body.

*Koromo.*

*Shiro Muji,* predominantly white *Kohaku.*

*Yondan,* four red patterns on body.

# Koromo

Translated as "robed," these koi typically have a red and white coloration with an overlay of silver, blue or black. *Koromo* koi are less common than other varieties.

Common examples:

*Ai-goromo,* white body with blue pinecone edging on red patterns.

*Budo Sanshoku,* white body with black scales on red scales creating a purple color.

*Sumi-goromo,* white body with black pinecone edging on red patterns.

# Ogon

This popular variety of koi has one metallic color which is gold or silver. These fish may possess normal, *doitsu* or leather type scales. High-quality *Ogon* do not have a black hue to the body. Some koi fanciers use the name *Hikari mujimono* for this variety.

*Ogon.*

Common examples:

*Gin Matsuba,* silver metallic scales with black pine-cone pattern.

*Kin Matsuba,* gold metallic scales with black pinecone pattern.

*Ogon,* gold metallic, or yellow-gold.

*Platinum Ogon,* white body with platinum sheen.

*Showa Sanshoku.*

# Showa Sanshoku (also known as Showa Sanke)

Sometimes referred to as simply *Showa,* this variety is primarily black with red and white markings, black on the head and black at the base of the pectoral fins. The latter is referred to as the *Motoguro*. This variety originated from the breeding of *Kohaku* and *Ki Utsura*.

## NAME THAT FISH!

Some koi delineations include:

*Aka:* Red

*Budo:* Grape

*Doitsu:* Scaleless

*Gin:* Silver

*Go-shiki:* Five Colors

*Haku:* White

*Hikari:* Metallic

*Kanoko:* Fawn-dappled

*Ki:* Yellow

*Kin:* Gold

*Kujaku:* Peacock

*Muji:* Solid

*Ogon:* Gold

*Rin:* Scales

*Sanke:* Three colors

*Shiro:* White

*Sumi:* Black

*Tancho:* Red spot on head

*Utsuri:* Reflection

*Yamabuki:* Yellow

Now, can you imagine what a *Gin Rin Tancho* would look like?

If you said a silver-scaled fish with a round red spot on its head, you'd be right! See the glossary at the end of this book for a more thorough listing of Japanese terms.

Common examples:

*Boke Showa,* faded in color with bluish appearance.

*Doitsu Showa,* mirror-type scales or none at all.

*Hi Showa,* red dominating over black and white.

*Kage Showa,* white scales with thin black lines around the edges.

*Kindai Showa,* white dominating over red and black.

# Taisho Sanshoku (also known as Taisho Sanke)

This popular variety is very similar to the *Showa Sanke* in its red, black and white tricoloration. Both varieties have been referred to as *sanske* by various authors, which means "tricolor." *Taisho Sanshoku* was developed during the Taisho era in the early 1900s. It differs from *Showa Sanshoku* in that these koi are primarily white, have black coloration on the back, the pectoral fins are colorless and black coloration is absent from the head.

Common examples:

*Aka Sanshoku,* mostly red.

*Doitsu Sanshoku,* small number of large mirror scales or no scales.

*Fuji Sanshoku*, metallic luster on the head.

*Kuchibeni*, red on the snout and lips.

*Tsubaki Sanshoku*, black pattern from head to back.

*Taisho
Sanshoku.*

# Tancho

The *Tancho* variety is fairly easy to identify in that it has a uniform white body and a red pattern on the top of the head. High-quality *Tancho* are judged by the purity of the white background and nature of the head pattern.

*Tancho.*

Common examples:

*Shinzo Tancho*, heart-shaped pattern on top of head.

*Tancho Kohaku*, white body with single red mark on head.

*Tancho Sanshoku*, white body with black patterns and red mark on head.

*Tancho Showa*, typical *Showa* with single red pattern on top of head.

23

# Utsurimono

Developed over 100 years ago, this two-colored variety is distinguished by a black background with white, red or yellow checkered patterns. The body is uniformly black with black present on the larger triangular pectoral fins and head.

*Utsurimono.*

Common examples:

*Doitsu Utsuri,* large sparse scalation.

*Hi Utsuri,* red body markings.

*Ki Utsuri,* yellow or orange body.

*Shiro Utsuri,* white body markings.

*Butterfly koi.*

The preceding koi varieties comprise those that are accepted in Japanese competitions. There are additional koi varieties that have been developed over the last few decades, but they are not eligible for Japanese competitions. The most popular nontraditional variety in the U.S. today is the Butterfly koi. This variety was bred in the 1980s from Asian carp and koi to produce elegant fish with metallic bodies and long, flowing fins. These koi are quite hardy, tolerant of colder temperatures and readily available to the koi enthusiast.

# chapter 3

# Purchasing Koi

Before addressing how to establish a healthy habitat for your pet, it is important to discuss the koi selection process that every new koi owner must ultimately go through. This will be an exciting and fun process because your koi pond will be established and you will be eagerly anticipating add-ing your fish to it. In general, koi are very hardy fish that can endure less than optimal conditions and varying amounts of stress. However, one of the most stressful periods for koi (and most vulnerable) involves their transportation and introduction into their new home. In this section, I will address the important steps of evaluating, choosing and transporting your new koi.

25

# Dealers

Koi can be purchased at a number of places, including pet shops, garden centers, koi farms, individual breeders and from other koi enthusiasts. Before you purchase your koi, be sure to select a source that you have thoroughly investigated. Koi clubs, Internet sources and exhibitions are excellent places to inquire about high-quality sources of koi and koi-related products. Try to visit all the available sources before you choose one or two with which to work. It is very important to establish a good working relationship with your dealer or breeder because you will need someone to advise you on many aspects of koi-keeping. You want somebody who maintains a good, clean business, has healthy fish and is always willing to answer your questions and spend time with you. He or she will be motivated by the desire to help you succeed in your hobby. Choose someone who shares your passion; someone who will be consistently available to help. Try to avoid dealers who will not take the time to explain things or to provide the specific koi that you desire.

## QUALITY FACILITIES

Take care to look for the following at your koi dealer's facilities:

1) Clean display tanks with biofiltered, odorless water. Each display tank should have its own filter to prevent the rapid proliferation of disease throughout the store.

2) Quarantine tanks for new arrivals with a two-week minimum quarantine process.

Experienced dealers have oxygen on hand to add to the bags that transport your koi. Your new koi are going to be stressed when they are netted and placed in a confined space. Fish that are stressed consume oxygen at a higher rate than normal. Filling the transport bags with oxygen will ensure that your koi will have an ample amount for the journey home.

Koi specialists will have a wide variety of koi and koi products available in the store. Look for a good assortment of products, ranging from those that are time-tested to the new and innovative. This is generally a good indication that the dealer "keeps up with the times" and follows the koi-keeping profession closely.

It can take time to find a reputable dealer that will provide expert consistent advice and high-quality koi and koi products. You may need to work with more than one dealer so that all your needs are met.

## QUALITY KOI

Be sure to inquire about the origin of the koi. This is very important because the origin of the koi can dictate the quality and cost of the fish. Be aware that koi can technically be called "Japanese koi" and not necessarily come from Japan. Koi that are bred in Japan are generally of higher quality and cost more than those bred elsewhere, but this is not always the case.

### AT THE KOI STORE

Koi can be found for sale at pet shops, garden centers and koi farms. You may learn of breeders in your area through the Internet or by reading the advertisements in koi-related magazines. Before you buy any fish, shop around. Be confident that the seller you choose not only keeps high-quality fish in a healthy environment, but is also pleasant and helpful. The new hobbyist (you) are bound to have many questions (both before and after you purchase). Find someone with whom you are comfortable.

# Selecting Koi

By reading this book and others, you should have a general idea of the variety of koi that you find most pleasing.

Keeping your personal tastes in mind is very important when selecting koi because you will likely have these fish for a very long time. Don't purchase any koi that is available to you through a friend or because of a reduced price. Realize that you are making an investment in a pet that will grow, respond to you and provide enjoyment for many years.

*Find out where your fish were bred. The phrase "Japanese koi" does not mean that the fish was bred in Japan.*

# SIZE DOES MATTER

The size of your new koi should be considered when choosing them for your pond. Many experts feel that one should purchase only mature koi because the good and bad qualities of younger koi are not as apparent—koi can change appreciably as they grow larger. In general, the better the color and the sharper the pattern on a small fish, the more likely it is to lose quality than it is to improve with size. On a young fish, the red should be an orange/red, and the white will move from the abdomen to the back with growth. Gray in young fish will surface as black when they get older. These changes will affect the color pattern of your fish.

## KOI QUALITY: HOW IMPORTANT IS IT?

For the new koi-keeper, expensive, top-of-the-line acquisitions are best avoided. Know that your pond is well-established and healthy before adding any fish. By beginning with koi of average quality you can "get your feet wet" while taking less risk. Just like other pets, koi that don't win "Best in Show" make fine companions.

## START WITH "PET QUALITY" KOI

Choose koi that you find attractive even if they are not of a recognized variety. All too often, novice koi-keepers spend money for expensive Japanese koi that do not survive in the newly established pond. Keep this in mind when purchasing your first koi. Work out the problems of your new system before investing a lot of money in your fish. Finally, as you add new koi to your pond, vary your selection so as to provide new interest and color to your pond environment.

## MOVING TO "SHOW-QUALITY" KOI

Although I do not recommend that you purchase expensive show-quality koi for your first fish, there may be a time when your interest in such fish will pique. If you are looking for mature show-quality koi, there are a number of features that you must consider. Koi are judged on the criteria of shape, color and pattern. A well-shaped koi is symmetric, with a straight backbone, fins in proportion to the body and an abdomen more rounded than the line of the back. The distance between the dorsal fin and the tail should be one-third the distance between the front of the dorsal fin and the head region. If the dorsal fin is too near to the tail, it is considered an inferior fish. The head should be in pro-portion to the body and not too rounded. The cheeks of the koi should be solid and round, and the head should be without blemishes. The color should have depth and clarity, and all the colors should be of even hue. White should be pure and without specks, as should the red. A koi with bright orange coloring is

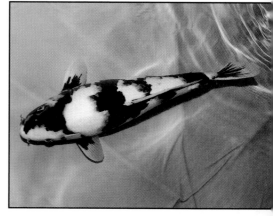

considered to be of better quality than one with purplish-red coloring. In most koi varieties, markings that are round are favored to those that are uneven or angular. The overall pattern should be well-balanced and consistent over the body of the fish. Borders between colors should be crisp and distinct with sharp edges. Finally, the skin should be lustrous and appear lacquered.

*Show-quality koi are judged on the basis of their shape, color and pattern. It is best to learn to care for lesser quality fish before you invest in "top-of-the-line" koi.*

## Selecting Healthy Fish

Knowing the quality of koi that you desire is an important aspect of selecting your fish, and evaluating the health of your selection is the other. Be selective when you get to the dealer. Buy koi only from healthy looking tanks with clear water, clean panes and no dead fish in the tank. Make sure that the fish you want appears to be in the best of health, with clear eyes, unblemished skin and full fins. If

### START OFF RIGHT—BUY ONLY HEALTHY FISH

Take the time to examine closely each and every fish that interests you. Is the fish active and bright-eyed? Is the skin clear and unblemished? Do any of the tank-mates appear to be in anything but the best of health? Although you should quarantine a new purchase before placing it in your pond, don't take chances.

the fish has any cuts, scrapes or fin problems, don't buy it. Watch for possible symptoms of disease, such as bulging eyes, white granular spots, cottony white patches, frayed fins or dull skin. Disproportionate bodies, large heads and pinched abdominal regions are all signs of sick or neglected fish.

*It is very important that you start your pond off right with healthy fish. Closely examine the koi that interest you for signs of disease.*

Watch the behavior of the fish. Healthy fish swim in a lively manner throughout the water column and are not shy. Koi that are gasping for air at the surface are not getting sufficient oxygen and are in a chronic state of stress. Even though you may be interested in a particular fish, inspect all the koi in that tank as well as those in other parts of the store. If other koi in the store are unhealthy, then it is likely that the koi of your choice has not been properly cared for. *Note:* If you bring home a single sick koi and introduce it to your pond, you threaten the health of all your koi.

## Bringing Your Fish Home

When you have selected your new koi, make sure that the dealer properly handles, bags and prepares the fish for transport home. The koi should be netted quickly with a large, shallow, soft mesh net and transferred to an appropriate heavy-duty bag filled with ample amounts of aerated water. Too much chasing and the fish will be too severely stressed for the transportation process. As mentioned earlier, the bag should be filled with oxygen before being sealed. If the fish is to be transported through a variety of temperature levels, then care should be taken to insulate the bag in a Styrofoam container so that a constant temperature can be maintained. This packing method should suffice for most short-term transportation to the home.

However, the longer the fish is in the bag, the more carbon dioxide and ammonia will build up in the bag.

Bacterial concentrations and disease agents will increase with time as well. Most importantly, the koi is likely to become highly stressed, rendering it vulnerable to disease. If your koi are to be bagged for more than a few hours, it is recommended that you add some common, noniodized salt to the water at a concentration of about 0.05 percent or 4 teaspoons per gallon. This will not harm the fish and will reduce stress associated with handling. For longer-term transportation, an ammonia detoxifier should be added to remove toxic forms of ammonia that will accumulate.

*In addition to its physical state, take a hard look at the behavior of the fish you like. It should be active and lively.*

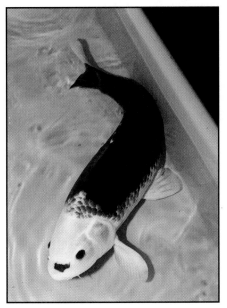

Some experts also suggest adding medications to the bag, but consult with your dealer for advice before doing so. Try to purchase your koi at a location that is not far from home, so as to keep time in the bag at a minimum.

Once your new pet koi are home, it is time to prepare them for their introduction into your pond. This will be discussed in subsequent chapters of this book. First we must discuss the habitat that your koi will happily live in, the koi pond.

# About

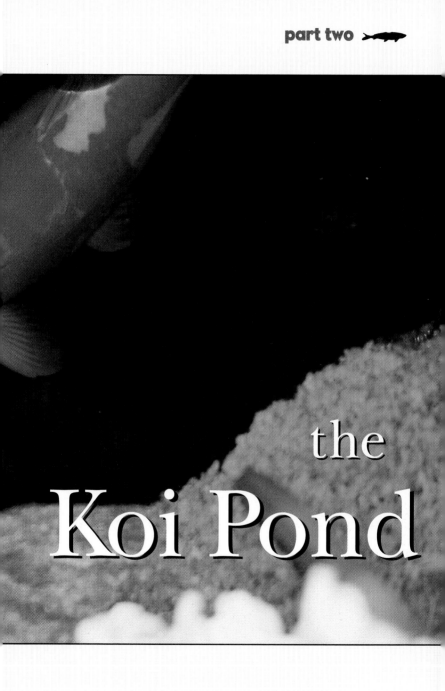

# the
# Koi Pond

# chapter 4

# Planning
## and Building
# Your Koi Pond

The large size of koi does not allow for fish other than small juveniles to be kept in a home aquarium, and these fish outgrow their home quite rapidly. The preferred habitat for koi is the garden or ornamental pond. Koi are cold-water freshwater fish that are capable of surviving in conditions that are less favorable for many species of fish. Koi are also temperate fish, which means that they can handle wide seasonal fluctuations in temperature. This hardiness, combined with their elegant beauty, has increased the popularity of keeping koi in backyard ponds.

Fish in their natural environment are subjected to many challenges in order to survive. Most of these involve natural processes of predation, feeding, reproduction and disease. Natural catastrophic events that alter water quality are rare and fish can generally avoid them by moving to other areas. In many ways, these fish are very much responsible for themselves. A possible exception to this would be fish that are living in areas assaulted by man-made pollution.

# Replicating Nature

When you take it upon yourself to set up a koi pond, you are accepting the responsibility of meeting all of the needs of its inhabitants. This entails maintaining high water quality, proper feeding, a balanced fish community of the proper density, and appropriate habitat and shelter to name a few. The koi are totally dependent upon you to meet their everyday needs. It's important to start slowly with your pond and develop your talents; you will learn a tremendous amount through your own experiences.

If you have maintained an aquarium in the past and are now planning to build a pond, you will see that there are many similarities and differences between the two. For example, there is generally no heater in a pond. It is important that you read this and other sources, such as *The Owner's Guide to the Garden Pond* by Roseanne Conrad (Howell Book House, 1997), before going out in the yard and simply digging a hole for your koi.

# Pond Design

Planning and designing your koi pond is critical to the process of creating a pond. Consideration must be given to the style of pond, placement of the pond, construction material, filtration and ornamentation, as well as other issues.

The style of pond that the koi enthusiast chooses is purely subjective, but must be considered at the start of the design process. It is generally recognized that there are two broad categories of ponds: formal and informal.

## FORMAL PONDS

Formal ponds follow geometric shapes and were typically built over the centuries in the gardens of Europe and the Near and Middle East. These ponds were designed to complement the architecture of the buildings built by the Greeks, Arabs and Romans. A formal pond is symmetrical such as a circle, square, rectangle, oval or octagon. They are often constructed of cement and, as a rule, do not contain many plants either in or around them. Although still popular, formal ponds look their best when surrounded by structured settings, such as formal gardens or older architecture. These ponds are popular with koi enthusiasts because they are simple to build and maintain. They are generally placed close to the home where the koi are well-attended and easy to see.

*A formal pond looks beautiful whether surrounded by plants or left barren.*

## INFORMAL PONDS

The other type of pond is informal or "free-form." This style was developed in China, Korea and later in Japan. There is very little symmetry to an informal pond and the shape is more natural. The informal pond can take the shape of a kidney or any other free-form object. Some are constructed with cement, but durable synthetic liners are the material of choice because they conform to the curves and angles of the pond. Typically, informal ponds are rich in beauty and garnished with waterfalls, fountains, elaborate plantings (both inside and outside the pond), wood structures, stones and a variety of ornaments. The informal pond setting, coupled with the beauty of koi, creates a symphony of natural elegance that enhances any home and enchants even the casual observer.

## THE CHOICE IS UP TO YOU

Whether you choose a formal or informal pond style depends on your personal preference, but be sure to choose a shape that provides good water circulation and eliminates the development of stagnant areas. Elaborate pond design is an art form in some respects. For those that are so inclined, there are companies that specialize in the design and construction of ponds. Reputable experts not only assist you with the development of your pond, but they also make sure that your pond contains the proper plumbing to maintain very high water quality. Koi clubs, koi magazines, pond and garden centers, and the Internet are places to seek out this kind of professional help in your area. Be sure to visit reference sites for any company that you are considering before committing your resources.

# Where to Place the Pond

Some feel that the most important part of installing your pond is selecting the site. This is a critical decision that must take into account a number of factors relative to water quality and pond maintenance.

Sunlight is an important aspect of siting your pond; it can be both beneficial and detrimental to your koi. Direct exposure to sunlight will elevate water temperatures in the pond to levels higher than koi prefer. In addition, too much sunlight will create unsightly algae blooms that degrade water quality and cloud the water. While small amounts of algae are beneficial to the pond by consuming nitrogen and releasing oxygen, excessive amounts will cause water fouling and oxygen deprivation. Every effort should be made to site your pond in an area of partial sunlight so that your koi will enjoy the heating effects and your plants will get sufficient light.

## TREES

*Partial sunlight
is best for plants
and for the water
in your pond.*

Care should be taken not to site the pond too close to trees because root systems will not only make it difficult to construct the pond, but will eventually do damage to the structure. Moreover, overhanging trees leach toxins and shed leaves that acidify the pond water, making pond maintenance more difficult. Insects that are attracted to trees will also find their way into your pond creating additional problems.

## SLOPE

Be sure to take into consideration the grade or slope of the land when you are siting your pond. The pond must be level, so extensive grading and sculpturing of the land may be required to achieve this. Take precautions to be sure that the area does not funnel water into your pond. Such runoff will destroy water quality by adding organic materials and toxic chemicals, such as fertilizers and pesticides, to your pond. In some cases, heavily sloped land can be used to add a waterfall to the pond system.

## DISTANCE

Many enthusiasts site their ponds close to their homes for several reasons. Ponds that are near windows will provide constant sources of enjoyment and an easy method for observing your fish. Your koi will get more attention if they are living close to where you are living. Logistically, a pond close to the home will be close to water and power sources as well. This will reduce the need to move water and electricity great distances, thereby reducing the cost of pond construction. Before siting your pond, carefully examine local zoning laws. You want to be sure that your pond will not be in violation of zoning restrictions *before* your start to build.

# Pond Size and Depth

## SURFACE AREA

All too often, the first pond of the koi enthusiast is too small. That is why every effort should be made to build as large a pond as possible at the start. Pond expansions can be an expensive and difficult task. A small pond is difficult to maintain and you are restricted in the number of koi that can be kept. Some experts recommend 150 square feet as a minimum surface area for a koi pond.

*This lovely public koi pond is a good example of the balance between surface area and number of koi.*

The number of koi that you will be able to maintain in your pond is directly related to the size of the pond and the surface area. Koi, like all fish, require adequate space to swim and sufficient oxygen to live; both are dictated by the size of the pond. The oxygen content of water is related to the surface area of the pond and the temperature of the water. Warmer water has less oxygen than colder water. Because ponds are maintained outside and most do not have heaters, the season and the time of day will have a significant impact on the amount of oxygen in the pond. There are times when oxygen is limited. The greater the pond's surface area, the more room for gas exchange at the surface and the more oxygen entering the water and toxic gases leaving the water. Therefore, the greater the surface area, the more koi the pond can hold. A general rule of thumb is 30 square inches of surface area per 1 inch of fish. Therefore, a 150-square-foot pond (21,600 square inches) can hold approximately thirty-six 20-inch koi. When making this calculation, always take into account the maximum size that your koi will attain and not the size that they are when you buy them.

## SITING YOUR POND

Many people want to be able to enjoy their pond from inside the home, as well as up close. It's a good idea to place your pond relatively close to your home. You will be visiting on a very regular basis (at least to feed your fish!) and you don't want maintenance to become a burden. Moreover, you will need plumbing and an electrical source to power lighting and filters—these are easier to provide when the pond is nearby.

## POND DEPTH

In addition to sufficient surface area, adequate depth is also a necessity. The depth of the pond required depends greatly on your local climate, but deep water is integral to maintaining healthy koi. The depth of your koi pond should vary in a shelf-like fashion. Ponds with a uniform depth pose problems relative to temperature fluctuations and predation. Deeper ponds do not have as much temperature fluctuation as shallow ponds, which is often more important than absolute water temperature. Deep ponds also provide better protection from predators, such as herons, raccoons and cats. Koi are healthier if provided with vertical swimming activity as well as horizontal swimming area. Deeper ponds will not freeze in the winter, thereby allowing you to keep your koi outside throughout the year.

Some experts feel that a pond depth of 8 feet is ideal for koi. However, because koi are naturally bottom-feeders, many feel that the enthusiast will rarely see the fish in a pond this deep. The shelf-style or terraced pond with gradually changing depth is a logical compromise to this dilemma. The shallow zone should not exceed 20 inches, sloping into water with a depth of 5 feet or more, depending on the severity of the winter. Shallow areas should slope at a steep angle into deeper pond zones. A deep central zone will accumulate debris that can easily be removed. The range of depths will serve multiple purposes. In the shallow zones, plants can be maintained and koi can be fed. In the deeper areas, koi can seek refuge from predators and extreme heat; they can hibernate below the ice during the winter months.

# Pond Materials

Over the centuries that koi have been maintained in ponds, the materials used to build them have evolved as new products were developed. For many years, the concrete pond was the only choice for pond keepers. However, recent technologies have produced new materials that are lighter, easier to install and less likely to leak. These include the pre-molded and flexible liners.

## CONCRETE

Concrete ponds were the standard for many years. They can be custom-built to fit any landscape, but the initial design and construction costs can be expensive. Although concrete is very strong and easily shaped, time may slowly take its toll on your pond. Climatic changes can eventual cause cracks to form and your pond will develop leaks. Repairs will be costly and the problem will eventually return. If you are interested in building a concrete pond, you must make sure that the walls and bottom are thick and that the concrete used is not porous. The bottom should be up to 12 inches thick and the walls at least 4 inches thick. Any concrete pond that is not of a simple geometric shape should be constructed by a contractor who specializes in such work. In addition, you must be sure to condition the pond over a three- to five-day period so that the excessive amounts of lime associated with the concrete will be neutralized. This requires the addition of phosphoric acid and continuous pH monitoring.

## PRE-MOLDED OR RIGID LINERS

The pre-molded liner is considered by many to be the preferred starter material for the novice, because of the ease of installation. However, be mindful that most pre-formed ponds are relatively small and you should provide a large habitat for your koi.

Pre-molded fiberglass ponds are expensive, yet very easy to install. These ponds are available in a number of formal and informal shapes. Overall, this pond material has a very long life expectancy.

The current preference in pre-formed (or rigid) liners, are those made of polyethylene. These black liners are very lightweight, heavy-duty and can withstand wide seasonal fluctuations. They are available in a variety of sizes and shapes. Polyethylene pre-formed waterfalls are also available to complement the pond. Drawbacks of this pond material is that the edges of these ponds can be awkward to work with, and usually require some creative efforts to hide. As with any pre-molded pond, care must be taken to make sure that the hole you dig accommodates the form very snugly. It is a good idea to line the pit that you dig with 6 inches of sand. As you fill the pond and the form settles, there will be some play in the earth beneath it.

## FLEXIBLE LINERS

More and more koi enthusiasts are building ponds using new flexible liners. Flexible liners are made from a variety of materials and have several advantages over pre-formed and concrete ponds. These liners can be adapted to any shape and they are available in many sizes, colors and thicknesses. Although flexible liners will tear on occasion, they can be readily repaired with a patch kit.

## *PVC*

Liners made of polyvinyl chloride (PVC) are inexpensive. However, they are easily torn, they do not hold up to colder climates, they are very susceptible to the detrimental effects of ultraviolet (UV) light and they have a relatively short life span of four or five years. This is not the preferred material for a pond liner and it is rarely used today for large outdoor ponds.

## Rubber

New synthetic rubbers are the preferred materials for today's koi ponds. The most common of these liners is composed of rubber sheets constructed of a synthetic polymer called EPDM (ethylene, propylene, diene, monomer) of a thickness of 45 millimeters. This material is manufactured specifically for pond use and is, therefore, safe for your koi. EPDM is also used for roofing material so make sure that when you purchase this product the words "fish friendly" appear on the packaging. The wrong product could result in harmful toxins being leached into your koi's habitat. Rubber liners are very flexible, mold easily to the form of your pond and are not susceptible to UV light degradation. Most of these liners have a long-term guarantee of ten to twenty years and a projected life expectancy in excess of forty years. If a tear should develop, patch kits are readily available.

*Flexible liners can be molded to any shape and are quite durable.*

Butyl rubber is another synthetic liner material that is not as widely available as EPDM. It, too, is very durable, and is typically 60 millimeters (rather than 45 millimeters) thick. Manufacturers claim that it will last as long as fifty years. However, butyl rubber can be more expensive and more difficult to work with than EPDM. Moreover, it is not recommended for use with plants.

Before installing these liners, be sure to place a layer of sand on the bottom of the pond to help protect the

liner from punctures by rock or stone. In extremely
rocky areas, it is recommended that you use a strong
fiber underlay for extra protection. Some pond keepers have reported using newspapers or old carpeting as
cushioning with good results. Because these liners are
a common component of your typical pond, some distributors sell them with pumps and filters as a package.

## Liner Size

It is not unusual for the novice to make the mistake of
purchasing a liner of a certain size and then digging a
hole of that size and finding that the liner is too small
for the pond hole. You must take into account the
depth of the pond when calculating the size of the liner.

First, determine the desired size and shape of your
pond. To obtain the proper measurement for the liner,
multiply the desired pond width by twice the maximum
pond depth, and then add 2 feet (1 foot for each edge).
Make the same calculation for the desired length of
the pond. The extra 2 feet are added to account for an
overhang of 1 foot around the perimeter of the pond.
You will also need to add separate liners for your waterfalls and any other pond elements that contain water;
these can be seamed to your main liner.

# Ornamentation and Decorations

There are a number of ways to make your pond and its
surroundings very beautiful. Some, like terraces and
islands, are generally part of the initial design of the
pond. Others, such as plants and ornaments, are simple additions to the pond.

## Terraces and Islands

As mentioned earlier in the discussion of pond depth,
terracing the pond from shallow to deep water in a
shelf-like fashion is an excellent idea. In addition to
providing a range of depths for your koi, this will also
provide areas for plants and other ornamentation.
Terracing is done during the building phase when the
pond is excavated. If your pond is already built and

lined and you want to add a shelf or terrace, then you can place stepping stones or bricks into the pond to build a shelf.

In a similar fashion, islands can be built or added to your pond as an attractive feature. The island can support plants or other ornamentation.

*Terraces provide a range of water depths for your koi and are a great place to show off plants. These pond builders construct levels as they excavate.*

## WATERFALLS AND FOUNTAINS

By designing your pond with waterfalls and/or fountains, you are not only adding attractive features, but you are increasing the health of your pond. Both additions move water and increase aeration, thereby benefiting the water quality in your pond. Before building your pond, carefully design where you want a waterfall or fountain placed. It is best if these features are tied in with your filtration pump.

## Building Your Pond

Once you have carefully designed your pond with the appropriate materials and features, you are ready to build a home for your koi. Although you can physically construct the pond yourself, be sure to seek the assistance of a certified electrician and plumber for the wiring and piping of the pond.

> ### YOUR POND IS YOUR CREATION
>
> There are a variety of decorations that you can add to your koi pond, and how you choose to decorate will depend on your personal taste. Bridges, ceramics and external vegetation will augment the natural beauty of your pond. Be creative and add features that aesthetically please you.

In most cases, your filter system will be piped and installed along with the pond. The principles and design of filtration systems are the topic of chapter 5. In this discussion of pond construction, it is assumed that you have chosen an efficient and properly sized filtration system for your pond and are prepared to install it.

## EXCAVATION

First, carefully lay out the perimeter of the pond with a rope or garden hose. Using brightly colored spray paint, make a line outside the hose or rope layout. This will serve as your guide throughout the excavation.

*In digging your pond, start at the perimeter and work toward the center.*

Using a spade or shovel, begin digging vertically around the marked perimeter of the pond. Depending on your pond design, now is the time to add your plant shelves. If you intend to conceal your liner under a coping shelf, dig this shelf first. In general, dig a coping shelf of about 12 inches deep by 12 inches wide. You may need to alter these dimensions to comply with the size of your coping material. Terrace the pond as you dig deeper, adding shelves for plants. In general, shelves are about 12 to 20 inches deep and 12 to 20 inches wide. Work your way toward the center, excavating the interior of the pond. Always dig a little deeper than the desired depth, because you are going to add a layer of sand or other protective cushioning on the bottom. If you plan on installing a waterfall, move some of the soil to that area and build the grade.

When the pond is excavated, be sure to check for rocks that may damage your liner. If you notice large tree roots, these, too, could pose a future problem. Tree root systems may ultimately damage a pond. If you encounter roots, you should consider moving your pond.

*Lay out the liner flat against the walls of the pond making sure that it hugs the bottom and the sides.*

Larger ponds should have an overflow pipe and a bottom drain to prevent problems associated with overflow. The overflow pipe, drain and external filter plumbing should be done at this time.

*Complete the coping shelf by covering it with stones.*

After excavation and plumbing, prepare the bottom of the pond by laying down the layer of sand. This will protect the liner from punctures. After filling holes, a 1- to 2-inch layer on the shelves and bottom should be sufficient. Smooth and firm down the sand layer.

Once the underlay is in place, the liner can be added. Unfold or unroll the liner and refold it in a fashion that makes it easy to install from the center of the pond. Lay out the liner flat against the walls of the pond making sure that it is flush with the bottom and sides. You may need to use rocks or bricks to hold the liner down as you work. It is best to have somebody assist you in placing the liner.

*When you've completed your work, you need to allow the pond water to be properly conditioned. This is a good time to do some landscaping.*

If you are adding a waterfall, now is the time to build it. Working with the soil mound left from the excavation, shape the waterfall so that a small pool at the top leads to cascading steps down to the pond. Be sure that

the waterfall is deep enough so that water does not spill over the edges. Once shaped, the waterfall can be lined and seamed to the pond liner. Stones can now be added to the falls at each tier to direct water and to conceal the liner. Be sure to properly plumb the waterfall during the construction phase so that piping will be concealed as well.

Now you can slowly fill the pond with a garden hose up to the level of the coping shelf. Complete the coping shelf with an appropriate coping material like stones or rocks. This will hide the liner and give the pond a more natural appearance. The coping stones should overhang the coping shelf by an inch or two. Add a layer of capstones around the periphery of the pond to conceal the edges of the liner. Trim excess liner, but be sure to leave at least 6 to 8 inches of overhang.

At this time, tie the plumbing together, which may include your filtration system, pumps, skimmer, UV sterilizer, bottom drain and overflow lines. Once the electrical systems are in place, the pond is ready to be turned on.

# Lighting

Both external and internal lighting will increase the beauty of your pond. By lighting your pond, you can showcase its various features, such as waterfalls and fountains. Exterior lights are easy to install and can be found in a variety of styles and sizes. Internal lights are placed underwater to highlight the pond. Be extremely careful when installing lighting. It is best to use a qualified electrician when installing lights in or very close to the pond. When it comes to lighting a pond, "less is more." Low-voltage spotlights have dramatic effects.

# Start-Up

Once your pond is up and running, you will have a strong desire to immediately add koi. Don't. Your pond may look ready, but it isn't. First, make sure that all systems are running smoothly, check for obvious leaks or overflow. Does the waterfall work correctly and is the filter system running smoothly? Scrutinize the pond for a few days to be sure that all is well.

## A LITTLE FISH IN A BIG POND

New pond keepers often don't realize just how big their pond should be. For your koi to thrive, they will need sufficient surface area and water depth. Start out with just a few fish in a big pond and add slowly to your collection. You don't want to make the investment of time and money needed to build a pond only to discover that your pond isn't large enough to support your fish.

Before you can add large numbers of koi, it is important for a pond to be conditioned. Like new aquariums, ponds need to go through a conditioning period during which the filtration system becomes established. This period is generally four to six weeks long. During this time, it is fine to add aquatic plants and a few koi or goldfish to the pond. You will be able to increase your capacity once high water quality is established. Frequent water testing will determine when your pond water is conditioned and your filter system is well established.

49

# Introducing Koi

Before introducing koi directly to your new pond, many experts feel that it is important to quarantine the fish for a period of two to three weeks. Quarantine prevents the inadvertent transmission of infectious diseases. Although your new koi may appear healthy, they

could be carrying a number of disease agents. Quarantine is especially important for the first koi that you add to your new pond. If the first koi are introduced to the new pond with a disease, treatment of the pond could be very detrimental to the conditioning process.

New fish are quarantined in a special quarantine tank that is set up for this purpose. The quarantine tank is generally 50 to 250 gallons in size, depending on the size of the koi. The tank must be well-equipped with a biological filter and a heater that maintains a constant temperature.

*Add the fish gradually as you begin to stock your pond.*

Water quality should be monitored in the quarantine tank to insure that the koi are being held in optimum conditions.

Before adding koi to the quarantine tank, be sure that the water temperature of the transport bag and the tank are similar. Place the transport bag in the quarantine tank to allow the former to equilibrate to the latter. When both are similar, open the bag and gently guide the fish from the bag into the tank without spilling too much of the bag's water to the tank. Be sure that the quarantine tank is covered to insure that the koi will not jump out.

Examine your fish during the quarantine period for signs of disease. Feed them lightly during this time and don't be alarmed if the koi do not feed immediately. They are recovering from the stress of shipment and may take several days to eat.

After the quarantine period, your koi can be transferred to the pond. Before doing so, make sure that the pH, water hardness and temperature of the pond water and the tank water are similar.

Again, feed your koi sparingly in the first few days until they settle down in their new home.

When stocking your pond for the first time, add your fish gradually, starting with just a few until the pond is well established. Continue to monitor water quality, making sure that your filter is working properly.

# Adding Aquatic Plants

Plants are a beautiful addition to any koi pond and they help improve water quality by removing nitrates and competing with noxious algae for nutrients. Plants provide areas for koi to hide and to spawn. However, koi are notorious for consuming plants, eating shoots and rooting around in the soil containing plants. Although considered by many to be incompatible, koi and plants can be maintained together if care is taken to select and protect the proper plants.

## Potting Plants

Plants that are added to the koi pond should not be planted in soil placed directly in the pond. One option includes potting them in containers specifically designed for pond use. By doing so, they can be readily moved for cleaning or overwintering. Potted plants can, however, present a few problems unless measures are taken to prevent koi from rooting around in the soil. Some pond keepers employ plant protectors that screen the plants, keeping the koi away from the soil. Others place a layer of small pea-sized gravel or lava rock on top of the soil to keep koi from getting to the plant roots. Others avoid plants that require soil and add those that are grown hydroponically, that is, without soil. If the latter is done properly, the plant can be

51

grown in a plastic mesh basket with lava rock about the size of golf balls.

Aquatic plants can be divided into three general categories: floating plants, shallow plants and submerged plants.

## FLOATING PLANTS

As the name implies, floating plants are surface plants that are either rooted in the bottom or free-floating altogether. These plants are relatively easy to care for and provide excellent filtration.

Unfortunately, koi will occasionally eat floating plants as soon as they are introduced into the pond. This problem can be remedied by using floating flora islands. These are made of fine mesh netting around a foam frame that you can anchor or allow to float free. The plants will pro-

*Water hyacinth is a beautiful addition to the koi pond, even when not in bloom!*

vide shelter and shade to the koi, while any roots that grow through the netting can be consumed by the koi without harming the plants. Floating plants that are recommended for koi ponds include:

### *Water hyacinth* (Eichornia crassipes)
Water hyacinth is a large flowering aquatic plant with intense lavender-blue flowers that stand in clusters well above its waxy green leaves and bulb-like stem. This is a cold-sensitive plant that must be taken indoors for wintering in colder climates.

### *Water lettuce* (Pistia stratiotes)
This rosette-shaped plant is medium green in color and has a somewhat compact mass of roots. It is an invasive plant that can rapidly fill a pond by the end of the growing season.

## Water lilies (Nymphaea spp.)

Water lilies are by far the most popular of the aquatic plants, possessing beautiful leaves and an abundance of flowers. There are two general types of water lilies: hardy and tropical; both are readily available for the koi pond. Hardy varieties are the best choice for the novice pond keeper because they are easy to grow and can overwinter in the koi pond. There are over 250 species of hardy water lilies in color choices of white, red, pink, yellow, cream and peach. Most hardy water lilies float on the surface of the water, but some will actually rise above the surface with the support of their strong stems. Tropical water lilies are not tolerant of the cold and should be treated as annuals. They also tend to be more expensive than their hardy cousins. These water lilies come in a larger variety of colors: deep purple, lavender, magenta, deep red, burgundy, cream, white, peach, salmon and green.

*Everyone loves water lilies, and the variety of water lilies for your pond is almost endless.*

Water lilies can be planted in pots or placed in floating baskets. New plants should be anchored in pots and placed in shallow areas of the pond until they are established. They can then be progressively moved into deeper areas as they grow.

## Lotus (Nelumbo spp.)

This large-leafed plant resembles the water lily, but possesses a much larger flower. They are relatively easy to grow and require little care and maintenance. Their rapid growth rate makes them generally suitable for larger koi ponds, but dwarf varieties are available for smaller ponds. Like tropical water lilies, lotus plants are intolerant of the colder climates and should be moved indoors for overwintering.

## SHALLOW PLANTS

These plants grow in shallow water with most of the plant exposed above the surface. They tend to produce lush vegetation and are attractive additions to the koi pond when scattered along the margins. Shallow plants prefer to keep their roots wet, but do not care for total immersion. The variety of shallow plants, sometimes referred to as marsh and bog plants, is terrific. Common shallow plants for the koi pond include:

### *Arrowhead plant* (Sagittaria latifolia)
This plant has spikes of white flowers accented by dark green arrow-shaped leaves.

### *Pickerel weed* (Pontederia cordata)
Pickerel weed is ideal for the pond margin. It has heart-shaped leaves that penetrate the surface and blue flowers on short spikes.

### *Umbrella plant* (Cyperus alternifolius)
These tropical water plants are intolerant of colder climates and must be moved indoors for overwintering. Their long stems and umbrella-like leaves make them an attractive addition to the margin of the pond.

### *Water iris* (Iris *spp.*)
The aquatic iris is a flowering marginal plant that blooms in the spring for about one week. Their sword-like leaves add height and texture to the pond. They are relatively tolerant of colder climates. Several varieties of many colors are available for the koi pond.

## SUBMERGED PLANTS

Submerged plants are often referred to as "oxygenators" because they play a role in combating algae growth by consuming excess nutrients, like nitrate. As implied by the name, these plants grow below the surface of the water and are rooted on the bottom. Although they are excellent for water quality, they are easily uprooted and eaten by koi unless the measures outlined above are taken to protect the plants. Common varieties of these plants include:

## *Cabomba (*Cabomba *spp.)*

Cabomba has fans of purple-backed green flowers with white flowers that bloom in the summer months. This hardy plant is tolerant of temperate climates.

*The right number of plants will soften the edges of the pond while not interfering with your enjoyment of the fish.*

## *Anacharis* (Elodea canadensis)

This bright green, lush, fern-like plant is the most common of the submerged plants. Fish particularly like to forage on this plant so care should be taken to protect it. Anacharis is a hardy plant and is relatively tolerant of colder climates.

## PLANT DENSITY

If you choose to add plants to your koi pond, do not overcrowd it with too many. You want to be able to clearly see and enjoy the water and the fish. Carefully design your pond with plants that soften the edges and floating plants that cover about 60 or 70 percent of the pond's surface. Submerged plants should be stocked at a density of one plant per 2 square feet of space.

# chapter 5

# Water Quality and Filtration

The most important requirement of healthy koi is clean water. Generally, fish in their natural environment are continuously exposed to an open system of fresh water. Products of respiration and digestion are swept away and naturally filtered by the environment. In contrast, fish housed in a pond live in a closed system where products of respiration and digestion remain until they are removed. The piece of equipment that removes toxic substances from the pond is the filter. Before examining filtration and the types of filters available to the pond keeper, it is important to understand the attributes of water quality and the natural wastes of fish. The pond keeper must be concerned with many aspects of water quality.

Freshwater fish have adapted to a wide variety of habitats around the world, and each species has its own water preferences. Koi are considered to be a very hardy species that is tolerant of differing water conditions. However, great care must be taken to avoid large or rapid changes in your pond's water chemistry. Two very important parameters that characterize the quality of your pond water and that need to be monitored include pH and hardness.

## pH

The amount of acidity in the water is referred to as pH. The pH scale ranges from 0 to 14 with a pH of 7 being neutral, a pH of 1 being very acidic and a pH of 14 being very alkaline. This scale is logarithmic, meaning that each number is ten times stronger than the preceding number. For example, a pH of 2 is ten times more acidic than a pH of 3 and 100 times more acidic than a pH of 4.

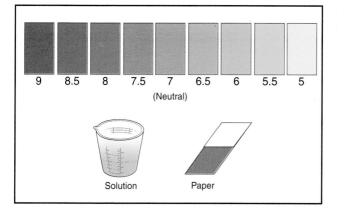

| 9 | 8.5 | 8 | 7.5 | 7 | 6.5 | 6 | 5.5 | 5 |

(Neutral)

Solution          Paper

*Determining the pH of your pond water can be done with a simple test kit available at most pond dealers. Results may look something like this.*

The acidity of water, and hence its pH, is influenced by a variety of factors that include the amount of carbon dioxide and fish wastes in the water. In general, koi are quite tolerant of various pH levels. Commercial pH test kits are very simple to use and available at most pond dealers. This water parameter should be monitored every week or two to detect any changes. In general, pH should be maintained between 6.8 and 8.0, and great fluctuations should be avoided. In contrast to tropical fish aquariums, low pH is rarely a problem in outdoor ponds unless runoff and rainwater contribute significantly to the pond. The pH of ponds with a considerable amount of plant life, particularly algae, will often fluctuate in a range of 7.0 to 11.0. In this situation, resident koi are stressed, but they will survive. However, new fish added to the pond frequently die after their introduction to the water, as rapid changes in pH will result in shock. Juvenile koi are more sensitive to pH changes than adults. If your pH exceeds the recommended range on a continual basis, it should be adjusted using commercially available buffers. These adjustments should be made slowly, never exceeding more than 0.2 units per day.

## Water Hardness

The amount of dissolved mineral salts, namely calcium and magnesium, will determine the water's hardness. Water with high concentrations of salts is referred to as hard, while low levels would be indicative of soft water. Hardness is measured with the degrees of hardness scale (dH), which ranges from 0° to over 30°, with 4° to 8° reflecting soft water and 18° to 30° reflecting hard water. This can also be expressed in parts per million (ppm)—soft water is less than 75ppm and hard water is within 150ppm to 300ppm.

Koi prefer moderately hard water in the range of 50ppm to 150ppm. You should use a commercially available hardness test kit to monitor your pond water, particularly in areas where the tap water is soft.

> ### MONITOR YOUR POND WATER
>
> Healthy koi are likely to remain healthy if their water is kept clean and balanced. Make a point to regularly check the pH and hardness of your pond water. Although koi are relatively resilient fish, they will become stressed, ill and may even die if their water conditions are not properly maintained.

## The Nitrogen Cycle

Koi, like all fish, are living creatures that obtain energy from food and burn that energy with the help of oxygen which they respire (breathe) from the water. However, these processes generate waste products that are returned to the environment via the gills and the anus. These wastes are primarily carbon dioxide and nitrogenous compounds, such as ammonia. In the closed system of the pond, these wastes must be removed or they will alter pH, predispose fish to disease, reduce normal growth and damage delicate gills. Carbon dioxide generally leaves the water through aeration at the surface or through photosynthesis by pond plants. Toxic nitrogenous compounds are converted to less toxic compounds via the nitrogen cycle.

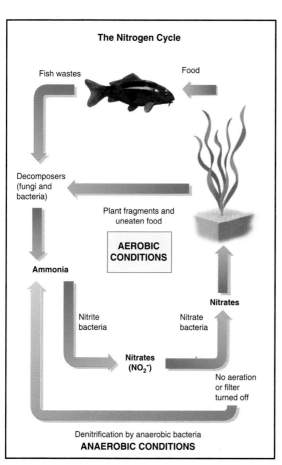

*The nitrogen cycle.*

## THE CYCLE OF NATURE

In nature, the nitrogen cycle involves the conversion of toxic nitrogenous wastes and ammonia into harmless products by bacterial colonies. In short, species of bacteria convert solid wastes excreted by fish into ammonia, ammonia into nitrite and nitrite into nitrate. Nitrate is then utilized by plants as fertilizer or converted to nitrogen gas and removed from the water.

## THE CYCLE IN YOUR POND

A healthy pond depends greatly on the nitrogen cycle to reduce toxic ammonia into less toxic nitrogen compounds. In most pond systems, nitrate will slowly accumulate in the water because the amounts of plants and bacteria necessary to utilize nitrate or convert it to nitrogen gas are lacking. These nitrates must eventually be removed, and this is done during frequent partial water changes.

When conditioning a pond, it is important to monitor the levels of ammonia, nitrite and nitrate to determine when the conditioning period is over. You should continue to test your pond water periodically to be sure that nitrogenous wastes are not accumulating to dangerous levels. Your dealer sells test kits that determine the levels of the compounds in your pond.

# Filtration

In natural systems, nitrogen compounds are readily removed from the fish's habitat. In the pond, this is accomplished by the filtration system. There are three basic methods of filtration: mechanical, chemical and biological.

Mechanical filtration physically removes suspended particles from the water by passing it through a fine filter medium, which sifts out the particles. Chemical filtration involves the chemical treatment of water to remove toxic substances. Biological filtration utilizes the nitrogen cycle to remove toxic compounds from the water and is essential to every koi pond. Most filters in use today provide all three kinds of filtration to a certain degree, but by far the most important kind of filter to purchase is the bio-filter.

# THE BIO-FILTER

Biological filters use a substrate, such as sand, gravel or bio-balls, to support bacterial colonies essential for water purification. The key to successful filtration is surface area—the greater the surface area, the higher the population of nitrifying bacteria, and the better the filtration. The better the filtration, the greater the carrying capacity of the system and, hence, the more koi you can successfully keep in your pond. An operational bio-filter does not need to be cleaned more often than once or twice a year. If you clean it, you actually kill the bacteria that are essential to the effectiveness of the filter. Bio-filters do not work properly in temperatures lower than 55°F, so they are generally shut down during the winter months. Otherwise, they are left running continuously twenty-four hours per day.

Biological filters can be located either inside or outside the koi pond. The undergravel filters are impractical for the koi pond because they clog easily and koi tend to root around in the bottom.

## Bio-Filters for Inside the Pond

Common inside filters are simple in design and are usually used in smaller ponds. They generally consist of a small box containing a pump to move the water through filter media like gravel or sand. The pump used by these smaller systems is submersible, which means that it is placed in the pond. Make sure that you choose a properly sized pump for your pond if you plan on using this type of filtration system. The pump should have a flow rate that is able to "turn over" the pond volume every three hours. In general, inside filters provide good mechanical filtration and some biological filtration, but their efficiency is very limited.

## Bio-Filters for Outside the Pond

If you intend to maintain a larger pond, you will require a more advanced filter design. The most popular filter used by koi enthusiasts is the outside biological filter. If properly designed, the outside filter provides excellent mechanical, chemical and biological filtration. The design of the outside filter is very similar to that used for most swimming pools. Water is drawn from the pond, pumped through filter media and returned to the pond. Intake ports can include surface skimmers, bottom drains and side-mounted drains. Water is purified by the filter and returned to the pond via outlet pipes, fountains and waterfalls, which provide aeration as well. The advantages of outside filters are that they are efficient and they are easy to build and maintain.

## Bio-Filter Design

*Your koi will thrive in a pond with a good filtration system. Removing waste and debris is critical for the health of your fish.*

Three kinds of bio-filter designs have been developed over the years: down-flow, up-flow and lateral flow bio-filters. In the down-flow (or gravity-fed) system, water is drawn from above through heavier waste that accumulates on top of the filter media. This causes clogging of the media over time leaving only a few channels where water can flow through the filter. Surface area is therefore diminished. Similar effects occur in the up-flow (or reverse flow) system where water is directed up through the filter media. In the lateral flow system, water flows laterally and heavier wastes drop to the bottom of the filter where it

can be drained off periodically. Channeling will not occur in the lateral flow system and the filter will work more efficiently.

## Bio-Filter Media

The most important part of the bio-filter is the filter media, the surfaces that house the nitrifying bacteria. A large variety of media have been employed by koi enthusiasts over the years. Remember, the best filter media provides a lot of surface area. Selection of the proper shape and size of the filter media is critical to its efficient function. The most commonly used medium is gravel that is graded by size. That is, fine gravel is placed on top of a coarser layer in the filter. The smaller sized gravel provides more surface area near the surface of the filter bed where most of the nitrifying activity takes place. This layering provides excellent filtration. The total filter bed should be about 2 to 3 feet deep, with the finer gravel on top and the larger rocks on the bottom.

Gravel is not the only substrate that can be used in the bio-filter. A number of media have been employed. Lava rock, canterbury spar, coke, perlag, flocor, plastic pot scrubbers, hair curlers and plastic bio-balls have been used effectively as filter media by koi enthusiasts.

Ultimately, your filter design will depend greatly on the design of your koi pond. I strongly recommend that you use the guidelines above and purchase a manufactured filter system with the advice of your dealer. Building your own bio-filter can be both a challenge and a risk that the novice is wise to avoid.

## SKIMMERS

*Skimmers remove algae and debris that collects on the water's surface. For a large pond, a skimmer is a must.*

Skimmers are generally employed in ponds that are larger than 6 feet in diameter. Skimmers pull water from the surface of the pond and deliver it to a filtration system. In doing so, they remove film, floating algae and other materials that often collect on the pond's surface. A collecting basket connected to the pond skimmer will allow for floating debris to be readily removed before it reaches and over-burdens the filter.

## ULTRAVIOLET STERILIZERS

Ultraviolet (UV) sterilizers are routinely used in large aquariums to kill algae, parasites and bacteria. Although not an essential piece of equipment for your pond, the UV sterilizer can be useful if the correct kind is employed. The keys to the successful operation of a UV sterilizer are flow rate and wattage, which differ by manufacturer. If you choose to use a UV sterilizer, consult with your dealer to select the proper one for your pond. Remember that the efficiency of the sterilizer will diminish over time and even though the light is lit, it may not be emitting enough to be effective. UV sterilizers should be placed after your bio-filter and should be cleaned regularly. They will cure a green water problem, but they are expensive and may be considered optional for the new koi pond keeper.

*Waterfalls not only add to the pond's beauty—they also serve as a great aeration device.*

# Aeration

It is important that your koi pond be properly aerated so that a high concentration of dissolved oxygen is maintained for your fish and filter bacteria. Fish need to have a good amount of oxygen available for respiration. This is especially critical for ponds that are maintained at their fullest carrying capacity of fish. Good aeration will increase circulation in the pond, promote oxygen exchange at the surface and increase the escape of carbon dioxide, carbon monoxide and free ammonia from the pond. In addition, this increase in circulation will act to mix all the pond levels so that a uniform temperature is maintained throughout the pond.

Although most filters provide water circulation and aeration to the pond, it is a very good idea to direct your water flow to aerating features, such as waterfalls and fountains, in your pond. Supplemental pumps can be added to larger ponds to circulate water and provide aeration. It is important to circulate all the water in the pond and to prevent the development of stagnant areas. Your dealer sells these pumps to achieve your aeration needs.

# Algae

Throughout this book, I have intermittently referenced algae as a pond nuisance that should be controlled. What exactly is algae, and do all algae cause problems for your pond?

Algae are actually plants that belong to the class known as *Thallophyta*. They are relatively simple plants that range in size from the one-celled microscopic types to large seaweed that grow to over 230 feet. Algae are also very hardy plants that have a tremendous reproductive capacity. They can enter your pond as algal spores born by the air, or can be carried by new plants and snails.

Most species of algae occur in the waters and, like fish, have adapted to all kinds of water conditions. In your pond, they can be found on the surface, suspended in the water or on the surfaces of rocks, gravel and pond decorations. There are four groups of algae that are most troublesome to the pond keeper.

## GREEN ALGAE

Green algae are the most common of the freshwater algae. This group contains one-celled and multicelled species. The one-celled green algae, such as *Chlorella,* are not visible to the naked eye but appear as a green cloudiness in the water. These will sometimes form a green film. Multicelled species, including *Volvox,* will also cause the water of your pond to look green. Green algae species like *Spirogyra* form a filamentous mass in the pond, while others form green threads attached to rocks and plants.

## DIATOMS

Diatoms proliferate in ponds with high nitrate levels. Diatoms form a brown slime on the gravel, rocks and decorations. Heavy concentrations of diatoms will discolor the water.

## Whip Algae

These single-celled species have tails or whips that they use to propel themselves through the water. These plants don't ordinarily affect the pond because they require such high nitrogen levels that the pond is usually stagnant by the time they proliferate. Water chemistry problems should be corrected before these species can take over.

## Blue-Green Algae

Blue-green algae are actually in a class of their own because they possess characteristics of both algae and bacteria. In your pond, blue-green algae form a dark green gelatinous mat on rocks, gravel and plants. If allowed to proliferate, they will smother the pond. High nitrate levels and bright light feed these algae, which can survive in both acidic and alkaline water. They are also capable of producing toxins that will poison your koi.

## Coping with Algae

In low levels, algae can be somewhat beneficial to the pond, providing the same benefits as plants. They supply oxygen during the day as a by-product of photosynthesis, and they consume nitrogenous compounds like nitrate, which normally build up in the pond. Koi consume algae, so they provide an additional food source for your fish. Unfortunately, when conditions are right, the algal population in your pond can explode, creating problems. Excessive algal growth will overrun a pond unless water quality is properly maintained. Rapid multiplication of algae depletes trace elements that are required by other plants. In warm conditions, algae will rapidly deplete the oxygen in your pond at night.

High nitrate levels and sunlight will promote algal growth. Avoiding these conditions and using a UV

---

**ALGAE CONTROL**

A little algae won't hurt your pond. Algae supplies oxygen to the pond water and your koi will nibble on it. Algae is less likely to "take over" your pond if you practice partial water changes and use a UV sterilizer. A good filter system and a proper load of fish will also help to keep algae in check.

sterilizer will minimize algae as a pond nuisance. If you seem to have excessive algal growth, there are several measures that you can employ to reduce the presence of algae in the pond.

- Use a UV sterilizer.

- Keep the pond well-planted; nitrates will be consumed by healthy aquatic plants instead of being available for algae.

- Make sure that all rocks, plants, decorations and gravel going into the pond are free of algae.

- Remove excess nitrates that will fuel algal growth by carrying out partial water changes in a timely fashion.

Don't become obsessed with algae to the point where you feel that all algae must be removed from the pond. I guarantee you that this is simply something that can't be achieved. A little algae does not cause an unhealthy environment. Expect to live with algae in your pond.

# Pond Care
## and
# Maintenance

Once your koi pond is well-established and your koi are healthy and happy, you may want to become complacent. However, it is time to think about continuous care and maintenance of your small pond ecosystem to insure the continued health of your pets. A well-established pond does not need a lot of maintenance, but you must keep it clean and free of waste and debris.

As previously mentioned, it is very important to test and monitor the quality of your pond water and, therefore, the efficiency of your filter. At least once a week, test your pH, hardness, ammonia, nitrite and nitrate levels. If there are any sudden changes in the pond chemistry, something is wrong and measures need to be taken before your koi suffer.

Check your bio-filter regularly and gently rinse heavy debris and waste materials from it. Filter pads can be easily hosed off and returned to the filter within a few minutes. The pump should be checked for clogging. These procedures take just a few minutes but will guarantee the health of your system.

Water will continuously evaporate from the pond, so you should add water with your garden hose on a periodic basis. Waterfalls, fountains and high temperatures will cause higher rates of evaporation. You cannot control the amount of water that evaporates, so be sure to watch the pond's water level.

## Cleaning the Pond

The most important aspect of pond maintenance is keeping it clean of debris and waste. When left in the pond, waste will cause rapid water degradation that will adversely affect your koi. Routinely remove leaves that enter the pond. Use a pond vacuum to remove any fine silt or dirt that collects on the bottom of the pond. A pond vacuum can be purchased at your pond dealer or at a pool dealer. They are usually driven by a garden hose and can be very effective at sucking up debris. If you have a bottom drain, this can be opened periodically to remove dirt.

> ### NATURE'S LITTER
>
> Regardless of your efforts to keep leaves and other debris from falling into your pond, some of "nature's litter" is bound to collect on the bottom. By regularly vacuuming the bottom with a pond vacuum, you help to keep your filter and pump in good condition.

## Seasonal Care

Depending on where you live, your pond and your koi will be exposed to changing seasonal conditions. For those living in southern climates where the weather is relatively consistent, routine maintenance will not change appreciably throughout the year. However, for those living in areas of dramatic seasonal climatic change, routine maintenance tasks will change with the seasons. The following discussion will specifically address pond care and maintenance in areas that experience seasonal changes in temperature.

69

# WINTER CARE

Koi are extremely tolerant of cold temperatures and will survive through the winter even in areas where ice forms. As water temperatures decline in the fall and winter, the activity levels of koi will diminish as well. You will not need to feed your fish during this time period.

As the koi become less active, they will generate less waste and the pond's filtration requirements will be decreased. Nonetheless, even in the dead of winter, koi will generate some nitrogenous wastes and you must continue to remove them or allow them to escape from the surface. Thus, measures must be taken during the winter months to prevent the pond from freezing over.

Keep an opening in the ice that will allow for oxygen exchange and the removal of toxic nitrogenous compounds. There

*Routine pond maintenance is not too demanding, but it is a necessity for the well-being of your koi.*

are a variety of methods that may be employed to prevent your pond from completely icing over. If your bio-filter can be kept from freezing, keep it running but bypass the waterfall if possible. Too much circulation will mix the deeper, warmer water with colder surface water and make the pond too cold. The small amount of water movement provided by your bio-filter will keep the pond's surface from freezing over. If your bio-filter is not plumbed for year-round use, you might need to shut it down. If this is the case, you can add a very small pump to the pond to bubble the water and keep it from freezing. Place the pump on one of the shallow shelves so that it does not mix the water layers. Some dealers recommend placing a small pool heater or a water tank de-icer in the pond, but these can be expensive and a bit excessive. Regardless of what you use to keep the pond from freezing, it is important to cover the pond with a pond cover or plastic sheeting. The cover will not only help insulate the pond, but will keep organic debris like leaves from degrading the water quality of the pond. This is especially important if you must shut down your bio-filter.

If your filtration system cannot withstand the extreme cold and must be turned off, be sure to clean it thoroughly before storing it for the winter. If you have a UV sterilizer, it too should be removed and stored during the winter months. Also, turn off, clean and store your fountain and turn off your waterfall. Lower the level in your pond by a few inches to allow for the natural addition of winter snow and rain. Be sure to remove any tropical plants for inside storage and clean the pond thoroughly, removing all waste and debris using the methods outlined above.

*Koi are a relatively hardy fish, and in most climates, you need not move them inside for the winter.*

In most climates, these measures will insure that your koi will survive the winter. However, in areas of extreme cold, koi should be moved inside for the winter. This will require setting up a rather large temporary aquarium in your home. For more information on how to do so, see *Setting Up a Freshwater Aquarium: An Owner's Guide to a Happy Healthy Pet,* by this author (Howell Book House, 1996).

## SPRING CARE

Spring is a great time to conduct a thorough cleaning. Some experts feel that this does not need to be done on an annual basis, but much depends on the condition of your pond, the filter type(s) and other factors. You can thoroughly clean your pond without causing great stress to your koi, because you should remove them from your pond at this time. You will need a holding tank like a child's small plastic swimming pool. You may even use your quarantine tank if it is large enough. Garbage cans generally do not provide enough room for your koi and should be avoided as holding tanks. Use your pond water to fill the tank and aerate it if you have a small pump. Be sure to cover it so that your koi do not jump out. Keep the holding tank out of direct sunlight so that the temperature remains stable.

## Removing Your Koi

Lower your pond level to facilitate catching your fish. Using a soft, shallow koi net, gently remove your koi one at a time and place them in the holding tank. In order to successfully remove all of your koi, you will probably need to get in the pond. Carefully, but quickly, examine each fish for signs of disease while it is in the net. You may quiet the fish by placing your hand over its head and eyes. Winter is a time when koi activity decreases dramatically. This not only includes the respiratory and digestion systems, but also the fish's immune system. When the water warms in the spring, the immune system is not functioning at full capacity and the fish are extremely vulnerable to disease. That is why it is very important to thoroughly examine your koi at this time for signs of illness.

*For a thorough cleaning of the pond, carefully net and remove each fish.*

## Spring Cleaning

After the koi have been examined and carefully placed in the holding tank, it is time to thoroughly empty and clean your pond. Scrub the pond walls and bottom with clean fresh water, but do not use any kind of soap or cleaning solution. Pump out all this water before filling the pond again. Make sure that your bio-filter is thoroughly rinsed if it has not been dormant for the winter. Closely inspect the liner to make sure that it is fully intact and free of tears. If your pond is concrete, check for cracks in the bottom and sides. Once cleaned and inspected, refill your pond with water.

## Starting Over

After your pond is filled with water, start up your filtration system and the other components of your pond (UV sterilizer, waterfall, fountain). You can also add your plants at this time. Basically, you should treat your pond like you did when you first set it up. This includes testing the water chemistry and making sure that it is ready for the reintroduction of your koi. If your bio-filter was not shut down for the winter, it will not require too much time to get it fully functional. If you did remove it for the winter, you should seed it with a bacterial start-up product to bring it up to speed as quickly as possible.

Reintroduce your koi to the pond slowly and methodically, as though you are putting them in the pond for the first time. You must make the water in the holding tank consistent with the new water in your pond. To do so, exchange a bucket of water from the holding tank with a bucket of water from the pond, but simply dispose of the water removed from the tank. Repeat this step every fifteen or twenty minutes, testing the pH and temperature of the water in both until they are very similar. When they are consistent, slowly reintroduce your koi one at a time. You may now start feeding your fish again after a dormant winter period. Be sure to start feeding slowly, providing a little food at a time.

> ### ANNUAL CLEANING
>
> You may need to perform a thorough, annual "spring cleaning" of your pond each year. If so, treat your pond as though you were starting it from scratch. Test your water chemistry and make certain that your filtration system is fully functional. Place your koi back into the pond only when you know that the environment is ready for them.

## SUMMER CARE

This is the time of year when seasonal temperatures are highest and you are probably enjoying your pond on a regular basis. High water temperatures and bright sunlight promote algal growth, so care should be taken to control algae. Make sure that all systems are running smoothly and properly. The filter bed of the bio-filter should be routinely raked once a month to minimize clogging. To do this, simply draw a rake over the surface of the filter bed down about 1 inch to break up the clumps of algae. This should be done throughout the year when the filter is up and running. Be sure that your UV sterilizer is running properly if you have installed one. Regularly clean out your surface skimmer and vacuum

*During the summer months, high temperatures and bright sunlight promote the growth of algae, so make sure that your filter and other systems are well-maintained.*

debris from the pond before it accumulates. Clean and inspect the pumps weekly as well. Summer is a time when debris and large particles constantly bombard your pond. If wastes accumulate, water quality will diminish and algae will flourish. If excessive algal growth occurs, remove it with a brush, but don't over-react to the presence of some algae in your pond.

## Water Changes

Finally, to further reduce the concentrations of toxic compounds in your pond, you should conduct a partial water change on a monthly basis during the warmest months of the year.

## FALL CARE

As temperatures begin to cool during the autumn months, your koi will slowly become less active. You should continue to monitor and test your water regularly and remove debris from the pond. Because fall is a time when many trees lose their leaves, your pond will be continuously burdened with organic matter. Try to skim the leaves from the surface before they drop to the bottom and begin to deteriorate.

Although you must continue to monitor your water chemistry and temperature, water changes will become less essential as the winter approaches. You will also want to reduce the amount of food that you are feeding your koi as the temperatures drop in late fall. *Note:* A dramatic decrease in water temperature will take a toll on your tropical plants and you may need to remove them prematurely if this occurs.

## Predator and Pest Control

Your koi pond will not only catch your attention but also that of other kinds of wildlife. Animals, such as birds, raccoons, cats and muskrats, will be attracted to the prospect of finding a free meal in your koi pond. Unfortunately, there is little you can do to keep these creatures from getting to your pond. By definition, your ornamental pond should be an aesthetically

*Steeply angled sides and well-planted shelves deter predators from your koi.*

pleasing habitat for you and your koi. Hence, the erection of any kind of fencing to deter these pests will diminish the tranquility and beauty of your pond. Note that some zoning laws require any pool or pond to be fenced, so fencing may simply be mandatory where you live.

If your pond is properly designed, predators will have a hard time catching your koi. Deep-water areas provide protection and shelves that are crowded with plants make it difficult for predators to access the fish. Steeply angled pond sides are also very effective at keeping pests out of your pond.

# Koi-Keeping

# part three

# chapter 7

# Feeding

# Your Koi

There are many considerations when it comes to providing food for your koi. You must not only consider the dietary requirements of your koi, but also the time of year and the water temperature. Although it sounds complicated, feeding your koi will probably become one of the most enjoyable aspects of keeping a koi pond. Koi are omnivorous, which simply means that they will consume a variety of foods of both plant and animal origin. In other words, they are not finicky eaters. However, because koi are cold-water fishes, their dietary needs will change depending on their activity level, which, as you know, depends on the water temperature. The size and age of your koi will also dictate how much they consume. Smaller, younger koi need more food to sustain their faster growth and higher metabolic needs.

Koi are different from many other species of fish in that they lack a true stomach. Digestion begins in the mouth where the food is ground by their molar-like pharyngeal teeth. The rate of digestion, like their dietary needs, depends on the age of the fish, the water temperature and the digestibility of the food.

There are many different types of food for your koi. Being omnivores, they will eat processed foods, red worms, whiteworms, earthworms, tubifex, brine shrimp, mosquito larvae, fruit flies, crab, lobster, oysters and clams, as well as canned vegetables such as beans, and fresh vegetables such as spinach, broccoli and cauliflower.

# Dietary Needs

Like all living animals, koi have dietary requirements for protein, fat, carbohydrate, vitamins and minerals. In their natural environment, fish will monitor their diet by foraging as needed. Although the algae in your pond will provide a source of food for your koi, they still rely heavily on you to meet their dietary needs.

## Protein

Protein is a major part of all animal tissue, and a constant supply is needed in your koi's diet to maintain normal growth. Proteins can be derived from plants, animals and bacteria. Younger fish require more protein in their diets than larger, older fish. Fry and fingerling koi should be fed diets that range from 37 to 42 percent protein, while adults require a diet of 28 to 32 percent protein. Protein is more difficult to digest than other nutrients. Therefore, most experts feel that less protein should be fed during the colder times of the year—early spring and late fall. However, a diet containing less than 28 percent protein will result in a deficiency.

Protein compounds are composed of smaller molecules called amino acids. It has been determined that ten kinds of amino acids are essential to the normal function of the body. A deficiency in any of these amino acids will result in low weight gain and depressed appetite. Care should be taken to insure that any commercially prepared foods contain all of these essential amino acids.

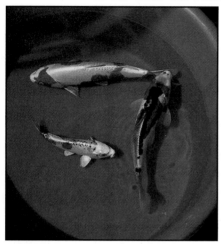

*Foods containing sufficient protein are essential to growth and to keep your koi looking great.*

## FATS

Fats, or lipids, are a primary energy source and an important component of internal organs and cells. They can be classified into two general types: saturated and unsaturated. The latter are more readily utilized than saturated fats. A diet containing too much saturated fat derived from pork, beef or poultry is not beneficial to koi. These fats end up as deposits in the internal organs of the fish, with deleterious effects. A diet rich in unsaturated oils is preferable. Most commercially prepared foods contain 5 to 8 percent fat, which is suitable for koi. Too much fat will cause excessive weight and fat deposits, while a deficiency will cause heart problems and fin erosion.

Do not purchase commercially prepared foods designed for other fish. Foods prepared for trout, salmon and catfish contain fats that are not good for koi. Make sure that your koi receive foods designed for koi.

## CARBOHYDRATES

Carbohydrates are another important source of energy for koi. Most commercially prepared foods are high in carbohydrates. Sources of carbohydrates include wheat, corn, barley and rice. Recent studies show that koi do not digest carbohydrates as efficiently as previously thought. Thus, foods very high in cereals should be avoided. Household foods unsuitable for koi include bread, dog biscuits and breakfast cereals.

## Vitamins

Vitamins fulfill the same important roles in fish as they do in mammals. They provide the necessary building blocks for proper metabolism. Vitamins can be either water-soluble or fat-soluble. The former include the B complex and vitamin C, while the latter include vitamins A, D, E and K. Vitamin deficiencies will cause a variety of disease symptoms, including loss of appetite, reduced growth, eye protrusion (exophthalmus) and bone malformation. Vitamins are readily destroyed when exposed to heat, air and metals. Much of the vitamin content of feeds can be lost due to processing and storage. Therefore, vitamin supplementation may be necessary for koi. The richest source of vitamins is found in green plants, vegetables, fruit and liver and fish oils. These foods should be used to supplement the diet of koi so that a vitamin deficiency does not develop.

### MEALTIME BONUS

For the owner, mealtime provides more than just the fun of watching your koi dine. This is a great time to examine your fish—are they active, and eating well? Try to get a good look at each of your fish, with an eye toward any sign of ill health.

## Minerals

Minerals provide the important building blocks for tissue formation and metabolism. Minerals can be derived directly from water or from food. The number of minerals crucial to fish health is extensive and typical examples include calcium, phosphorous, copper, zinc, magnesium, sulfur, iodine, iron and cobalt. Calcium and phosphorous are particularly important to koi, as deficiencies cause poor bone formation, slow growth and appetite depression. High sources of minerals include vegetables, such as spinach, kale and lettuce.

# Food Categories

There are basically four different categories of food: commercially prepared foods, frozen or freeze-dried

foods, live foods and household foods. Of these, live foods have the greatest potential to be harmful to your fish, as they can carry diseases or parasites. The following is a brief description of each category.

## PREPARED FOODS

Commercially prepared foods contain the three basic requirements of proteins, fats and carbohydrates. They are also supplemented with vitamins and minerals. These foods come in a variety of forms, but are typically pelleted for koi. Commercial pellets are very popular for feeding koi. Some are designed to sink and others designed to float—and they are available in a variety of sizes. Floating pellets are preferred by many koi owners because they give owners an opportunity to watch their fish feed at the surface. Floating pellets also allow koi-keepers to more effectively monitor the amount that they are feeding. Sinking pellets draw the koi deeper, may result in overfeeding and cause water quality degradation. Care must be taken to scrutinize the ingredients of the commercially prepared koi foods to be sure that they are properly balanced. Use the information provided above to be sure that all the nutritional needs of your koi are being met. Commercially prepared foods provide a good foundation for your fish's diet, but it should be augmented with other kinds of food so that a balanced diet is maintained. As mentioned earlier, only use feeds specially prepared for koi and not those for other species of fish.

Care must be taken when storing dry commercial feeds to insure that the quality of the product is maintained. Heat and moisture will degrade the product. Vitamins are very sensitive to high temperatures. In general, prepared foods should be stored in cool and dry areas for a maximum of ninety days. They should not be left open and exposed to the air while in storage.

## LIVE FOODS

Live food is an excellent source of nutrition for koi. However, many feel that live foods may carry diseases that can infect your fish. To insure against this, live foods can easily be obtained from your dealer or a pet store. This is a great deal safer than collecting live foods from another pond or lake.

The only two live foods that generally do not run the risk of carrying a disease are earthworms and brine shrimp. These are easily purchased and will provide an excellent addition to your fish's diet.

### Brine Shrimp

The brine shrimp *(Artemia salina)* in your local pet store probably originated in the Great Salt Lake area. They are one of the best sources of nutrition available for fish of any type. Of all the live food available, they are considered the safest because they rarely carry diseases. An added advantage to brine shrimp is that you can raise them yourself.

*Brine shrimp.*

To raise brine shrimp, it is best to follow the instructions accompanying the eggs. If these are lacking, follow these simple steps:

1. In a plastic or glass container, add 12 ounces of salt per gallon of water.
2. At the bottom of the container, place an operating aerator and keep it from moving with a stone.

3. Add 2 ounces of Epsom salts and 1 ounce of sodium bicarbonate to the container per gallon of water.

4. Empty a container of brine eggs into the mixture. Handle them with care because they are small and delicate.

5. With a water temperature of about 75°F, your eggs should develop into brine shrimp over the course of about two days. Continue to feed the shrimp brewer's yeast until the culture is completely fed to your fish.

## Earthworms

These backyard occupants are rich in protein and a readily available dietary change for your fish. You can either search for them after rain showers on lawns,

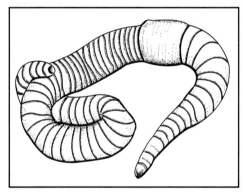

*An earthworm.*

around pools and lakes, under stones or you can cultivate them in your backyard.

To cultivate earthworms, take a few square yards of dirt in your backyard and throw burlap sacks over the tilled soil. Water the sacks every morning for one week until they are soaked. On the seventh day, lift up the burlap sacks and you will find earthworms. The best time to harvest is early in the morning before the dew has evaporated.

Earthworms live in and consume dirt, so it is necessary to rinse them and clean them off before feeding them to your fish. You don't want to introduce dirt into your pond if you can avoid it. After you get your worms, rinse them off, put them in a jar with holes in the lid and let them sit for a day or two in a dark, shaded area. Rinse them each day removing the dirt from their bodies. To feed them to your fish, it may be necessary to dice them up. Keep in mind the size of your fish when dicing your worms—larger fish can consume larger pieces than their smaller compatriots.

Make sure that no pesticides or weed killers were used in the area where you are cultivating or collecting your earthworms. Such chemicals will assuredly cause harm to your fish.

## Tubifex

These are long, thin, red worms, also known as sludge worms, that live in mud and are available from dealers. These live worms are an excellent addition to your fish's diet. Before feeding them to your fish, you must rinse them thoroughly in gently running water for at least one hour. If possible, rinse them for two additional hours. Tubifex require a

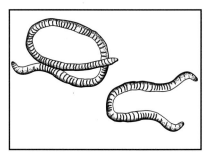

*Tubifex worms.*

lot of work and are a risky food because their habitat makes them likely carriers of disease. It is wise that you feed them to your fish only once or twice a month. Although it is possible to culture tubifex at home, I don't recommend it. This is a difficult task and, as tubifex should only be an occasional treat for your koi, not worth the time involved.

## Whiteworms

These white or beige worms are also known as microworms. You can buy them from your dealer in serving size amounts or you can culture them at home. Starter kits may be obtained from pet dealers or ordered by mail. It is best to feed these worms in small quantities to your fish because some feel that they can be fattening and constipating. To culture whiteworms follow these steps:

1. In a large tray or small shallow tub, place earth and mulched leaves.

2. Water the soil and place the worms on the dirt. Sprinkle breadcrumbs or spread sliced bread on the dirt. Some home harvesters use oatmeal.

3. Place a sheet of glass over the tray and cover the entire unit with a sheet or blanket. Make sure that the glass is touching every part of the container.

4. Place the tray in a damp place at room temperature and leave it alone for two to three weeks. The maturation period will depend in large part on the temperature.

5. When you unwrap the tray, the underside of the glass plate will be covered with whiteworms. Scrape them off and feed them to your fish.

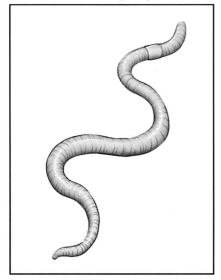

*Whiteworms.*

These cultures should remain fresh for about six weeks. If you suspect that the culture has gone bad, it is very important that you dispose of the entire batch and keep none of the worms.

### Daphnia

Also referred to as water fleas, *Daphnia* constitute another excellent live food for your fish. However, *Daphnia* can act as a laxative, causing serious digestive problems in your fish, so they should be fed relatively infrequently. You can buy *Daphnia* from your local pet store or easily culture them at home:

1. Fill a jar with an inch of topsoil, tamp it down, but don't pack it hard. Some suggest that you add manure or brewer's yeast as well.

2. Carefully pour some water into the jar until it is three-quarters full.

3. Place the jar in the sun for a week until you get a full growth of algae. Wait another week if there is not good algal growth.

4. Add the *Daphnia* culture and wait ten to fourteen days. After that time, water fleas are ready. To insure that the culture is maintained, never take more than one fifth of the culture. You must feed the culture so remember to add manure or brewer's yeast several times a week. This culture will only

last two to three weeks, but will provide two to three feedings a week for your fish.

## Drosophila

*Drosophila* are the larvae of the wingless fruit fly. Like the other live foods, you can occasionally buy them from the pet store or you can culture them at home:

1. Add agar and some smashed banana to water that you have boiled.

2. Let the mixture stand for a few days to allow it to jell.

3. Add some fruit flies, let them sit for two weeks and voila! You will have a lot of *Drosophila*.

## Bloodworms

Also known as two-winged fly larvae, these are usually in good supply year-round and can be purchased at your pet store. They are very difficult to cultivate at home.

## FROZEN OR FREEZE-DRIED FOODS

Frozen and freeze-dried foods offer the best of the live food without the risk of disease and without the hassles of preparing cultures. These include many of the live foods outlined above: brine shrimp, tubifex worms, *Daphnia* and bloodworms. In addition, mosquito larvae and krill are also available to the koi enthusiast in this form. Frozen and freeze-dried foods are a great convenience to the hobbyist who wants to provide variety without having to purchase or culture live foods.

## TABLE OR HOUSEHOLD FOODS

Table foods offer nutritional value and variety to the diet of your koi. Fresh, frozen or canned oysters, clams, mussels, crabmeat, lobster or bits of raw fish are excellent koi foods. Baked or boiled beans, steamed cauliflower or broccoli and boiled or baked potatoes are also healthful. Fresh spinach or lettuce is good for your koi.

Koi will eat almost anything that we eat, including beef, boneless chicken and pasta, but don't let your pond become a place to dispose of leftovers. These foods must be given in moderation. Remember, you are augmenting your fish's diet with these foods, not creating a staple. Household foods must be diced or shredded so that your fish can eat them. Don't offer your koi table scraps unless they conform to what is listed above.

## Diet and Color

The quality of your koi is largely determined by the quality of its coloration. The colors of your koi are dictated by the genetic potential of your fish, by the quality of your pond water and by what your koi consumes. You can control the first variable by selecting a koi that was bred from high quality parents. You control your water quality by how well you maintain your pond. And you can feed your koi specific color-enhancing ingredients to maximize its color.

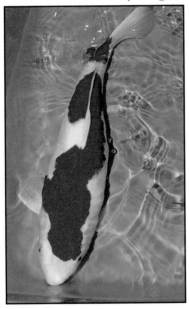

Naturally occurring pigments, such as those found in shrimp, marigold petals, plankton and the blue-green algae *Spirulina,* have been added to commercial koi feeds to enhance coloration. Koi will also feed naturally on the *Spirulina* that grows in your pond. This will enhance the red, orange and yellow colors in your koi. Many of the freeze-dried and live foods mentioned above, such as brine shrimp and *Daphnia,* contain high concentrations of carotenoid pigments, which are major pigments of the koi's skin. Be aware that koi that feed on too much color-enhancing food may develop too much color. This is particularly true for koi that are predominantly white. If this happens, simply reduce the amount of color-enhancing food that you are feeding your koi.

*By using commercial koi feeds that contain color enhancers, you can actually brighten the color of your fish.*

# How to Feed Your Fish

Probably the biggest challenge in feeding your koi is determining how much and how often to feed them. In general, many feel that it is better to feed too little than too much. Remember, koi are omnivorous and opportunistic. They will spend much of the day foraging, eating algae, plants, and insects that end up in the pond. Follow these guidelines when feeding your fish and you will develop a working sense of how much and how often to feed them.

1. Offer as much food as your koi will eat in five minutes.

2. Feed your fish in very small portions over the five-minute period.

> ### LIVING COLOR
>
> There's no doubt that the bright colors of koi contribute to their popularity. You can actually enhance the colors of your fish with the right foods. Commercial koi food contains ingredients with natural pigments that will in turn brighten the colors of your koi. But be aware of too much of a good thing: Your brights may get brighter, but your whites won't get whiter with injudicious feedings of color-enhancing foods.

*Healthy koi are good eaters and will scramble to the surface when you feed them.*

3. If you are home during the day, feed your fish over the course of the day in small portions. If you are not home, feed your fish at least twice a day at the same times every day, once in the morning, and again in the late afternoon. Younger koi need to eat more frequently, so if you can't be home to feed them midday, you might consider hiring a neighbor or pet sitter to look after your fish until they mature.

89

4. Always feed your fish in the same general area of the pond.

5. Don't overfeed the fish, no matter how much you think they need more food. Overfeeding will stress your fish and cause detritus to accumulate in the pond, degrading water quality.

## HOW MANY MEALS PER DAY?

Koi, like humans (and dogs!) need more frequent feedings when young than they do as adults. Koi fry will need to be fed all throughout the day (in tiny portions). As they mature, the number of feedings can slowly be diminished. As adults, koi should be fed at least twice daily.

Watch all your fish during feeding making sure that each gets its share of food. Remember, refusal to eat is one of the first signs of illness, so keep an eye out for fish that seem to have no interest in food.

Start with commercially prepared food as your staple and mix in a variety of foods as your fish acclimate to the pond. Don't crumble the food. This will add fine particles to the water that are not ingested but degrade water quality. Your fish won't have any problems biting and grinding whole pelleted food. Make every effort to remove uneaten food so that it is not left to decompose in the pond.

## SEASONAL FEEDING

The quantity and type of food you give your koi will change with the seasons. As the water temperature decreases in the autumn and winter you will need to pay attention to the amount of food that you give your koi. Remember that koi activity will decrease during this time and the food requirements of the fish will decrease as well. Feed your koi less and less as the temperature continues to decline. During the winter or when the water temperature is below 50°F, stop feeding your koi completely, regardless of how hungry you think they might be.

In addition, the dietary requirements of your koi will change with the decrease in temperature. You should alter the dietary composition of your koi's diet in the fall to help your fish prepare for the winter season.

Reduce the amount of protein and slightly increase the amount of carbohydrates and fat to promote fat storage for overwintering.

As the water warms again in the spring to about 60°F, begin feeding your koi in very low quantities once a day. As the weather continues to warm, slowly increase the food amount and frequency of feedings. Be aware that your bio-filter has most likely been shut down for the winter and must be re-established at this time as well. By feeding small amounts during this time, you will avoid overtaxing your filter with large amounts of koi waste.

In the active season of summer, a high protein diet is important to keep your koi healthy. This is the time to feed your koi at levels that will sustain high activity, but still be careful and do not overfeed.

If you are going to be away from your pond for up to a few days, the koi will be fine without food. For extended periods, make arrangements for someone to feed your fish.

# chapter 8

# Koi
# Health

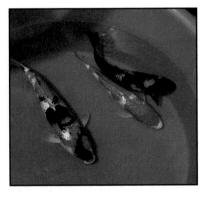

If you intend to be a koi enthusiast for some time, then inevitably one of your fish will become infected with some kind of disease. Freshwater fishes are subject to all kinds of maladies. Pathogenic organisms including parasites, bacteria and viruses are present in all ponds. Many are introduced with new fish and many are highly contagious.

The resistance of your fish is a critical factor in whether diseases actually take hold. Poor living conditions will weaken your fish, cause chronic stress and ultimately lower the fish's resistance, and fish with low resistance are most vulnerable to disease. This is why I have stressed the importance of maintaining a healthy pond for your pets. Stress caused by capture, handling, crowding and injury renders your koi vulnerable to disease. Koi are particularly vulnerable after a dormant wintering period when their immune systems are weak.

You may think you have done everything that you possibly could to have a disease-free environment in your pond, but even the experts experience these problems.

The first step to treating any kind of ailment in your pond is to recognize and identify the problem. You will be able to determine that your koi is not healthy by its appearance and its behavior. Because you have been spending time examining your fish while you feed them, you will be able to identify problems as soon as they manifest themselves. Telltale behavioral symptoms include no desire to eat, hyperventilation of the gills, gasping for air near the surface, erratic swimming behavior, lack of movement, rubbing of body or fins and twitching of fins.

External symptoms include a variety of physical abnormalities of the head, body, fins, gills, scales and anus. As I review the various diseases associated with koi, you will learn what the symptoms of each are.

# Commercial Remedies

It is very important that beginners use commercially available treatments rather than homemade remedies.

Some experts recommend treating with chemicals, such as malachite green or potassium permanganate. These chemicals must be handled in very exact dosages. If a fish is overdosed with one of them, it will kill the fish faster than the disease would have. Discuss all the possible remedies to a disease with your local koi dealer and let that person

> **HEALTHY POND = HEALTHY FISH**
>
> The need to maintain a clean pond with proper water chemistry cannot be overemphasized. If wastes are allowed to accumulate, your water quality will suffer and so will your koi.

advise you on the best commercial remedies that the store carries. If you are still not satisfied, don't be afraid to call your veterinarian and ask a few questions. If your veterinarian does not treat fish, he or she can usually recommend somebody who does. Finally, when you apply the remedy, make sure that you follow the directions exactly.

# Treatment Methods

The best remedy for disease in the koi pond is prevention. Sometimes, despite all your efforts and the application of commercial remedies, the fish will die. Nonetheless, if disease strikes one of your fish, there are several methods for treating it. These include direct pond treatment with therapeutic agents, the quarantine tank, the dip method and internal medication.

## DIRECT POND TREATMENT

The application of therapeutic agents directly into your pond is one way to fight off disease. It can be effective

against some diseases, but it is not recommended. In some cases, medications may be absorbed by the aquarium decorations, plants and filter media, or they may be toxic to filter bacteria. It is best to isolate the infected fish in the hospital tank.

## QUARANTINE

In chapter 4, I mentioned that new fish are generally isolated in a quarantine tank. In this way, the fish can be evaluated for signs of disease before introduction into the pond. This tank can also function as a hospital tank to isolate individuals that are suffering from disease—by

*One way to fight disease in your koi is to treat the pond itself—but this method is rather risky and not recommended.*

isolating fish that are ailing, you reduce the likelihood of the disease spreading to others in the pond. It will provide refuge to a fish that may ordinarily be harassed by healthier fish. The quarantine tank will make it easier to treat the koi without subjecting others to the treatment and it will make it easier to observe and diagnose the ailing fish.

The hospital tank may either be the same tank that you use to quarantine your new fish or you may want to set up a smaller tank that can be used specifically to treat ailing koi. If you do not plan on adding new fish to your pond in the immediate future, then the quarantine tank will suffice. However, it is not a good idea to use this tank to house diseased koi if it is frequently used for new koi acquisitions. Regardless, the tank used to treat disease-bearing koi does need adequate filtration and aeration, but plants and gravel should be omitted. Try to provide some kind of cover for the fish in the form of rocks or flowerpots as a source of security.

*Because new treatments are always being developed, research your options before taking action. You want to make the right choice for your koi.*

## THE DIP METHOD

The dip method involves removing the infected fish from the pond and dipping it into a bath containing a therapeutic agent or simply salt water. It can be very stressful for the fish. The dip is brief enough not to injure the fish, but long enough to kill the pathogen.

## INTERNAL MEDICATION

Some remedies need to be administered internally. This is usually accomplished with injection or by feeding the remedy to the fish. The former method is not recommended for the average home aquarist. Feeding the koi food that has been medicated can be very difficult as well. In many cases, the dosage is difficult to estimate, the fish is not feeding normally, and you cannot guarantee that the koi being treated is getting the proper amount of food. This type of treatment method

95

is, therefore, only marginally successful and should be avoided by the beginner.

# Common Treatments

A variety of treatments are available to the koi enthusiast faced with a diseased fish and new remedies are being developed every year. I recommend that you discuss your disease problems with your koi dealer for the latest in new innovative methods to treat your ailing koi.

## THE OLD-FASHIONED SALT BATH

The salt bath is the most time-tested cure-all of the fish world. Sometimes called the progressive saltwater treatment, it is undoubtedly the most common use of the hospital tank. This very simple treatment has been known to cure a number of fish diseases including ich, fungus, velvet and tail rot. Many experts swear by it.

> **WHEN IT COMES TO TREATMENT, KEEP IT SIMPLE**
>
> When treating a diseased fish, start with simple, less radical remedies. Often, you'll find that an old-fashioned salt bath will do the trick, rending a more aggressive (and potentially more risky) approach unnecessary.

You simply add 1 teaspoon of table salt (not iodized) for each gallon of water to the quarantine tank that houses your fish. Add the same amount of salt that night and twice the next day, again in the morning and at night. If the fish is not improving by the third or fourth day, add 1 more teaspoon of salt each day. On the ninth and tenth days, make progressive water changes and check for results.

## ANTIMICROBIALS

Antimicrobials are chemotherapeutic agents that seem to be the most effective way of treating common microorganisms, such as bacteria, fungi and viruses. This group of drugs includes some of the common antibiotics, like tetracycline. When possible, fish should be treated in a quarantine tank to avoid the effects of these compounds on a mature established pond. Regardless, don't expect miracle cures from these compounds because many have not been found to be fully effective against disease.

## PARASITICIDES

Parasiticides are medications used to treat parasites like leeches, copepods, tapeworms, protozoans and trematodes. A number of commercial remedies are available that target parasite infestations. Common parasiticides include malachite green, salt and metronidazole.

## EMERGENCY CLEANING

The emergency pond cleaning should be a very rare event and I don't recommend it unless the health of your koi and your pond has been severely compromised. If any of the infestations mentioned below strike several koi, you need to take drastic measures and perform an emergency cleaning. In this case, treat the pond as though you are performing a thorough spring-cleaning. Place all the fish in a holding tank and begin treatment. Then, turn your attention to the pond.

*If several of your fish become ill and the health of your pond is at stake, an emergency cleaning may be in order. Essentially, you must empty your pond and start it from scratch.*

This very simply involves starting your pond from scratch. It must be thoroughly cleaned and totally restarted. Throw out filter media and save as little as possible. Empty out the contents of the pond. Rinse the walls, the bottom and the filter with bleach. Of course, make sure that you rinse everything extremely

97

thoroughly. If you have any live plants, dispose of them, too, and don't use them for any other purpose. Replace the filter media, airstones and the like. In essence, you are starting over again because your pond was overrun by disease.

# Diseases, Infections and Parasites

There are literally hundreds of possible maladies that can afflict fish. Some are specific to certain species and some can easily be transferred between species. Not all are common in the average garden pond. The causes of common ailments may be bacteria, viruses, fungi or parasites. The following provides a general overview of those diseases you are most likely to encounter in your koi pond. For a more complete listing of tropical fish diseases and their treatments, consult the references in chapter 11.

> **GET EXPERT ADVICE**
>
> Hopefully, you established a good relationship with a knowledgeable breeder or dealer when you purchased your koi. You will usually find that your dealer is eager to help you succeed with your pond and your koi. Seek his or her advice if you believe that your koi is ailing.

## NONINFECTIOUS AILMENTS

Noninfectious diseases are generally caused by poor water quality, inadequate nutrition, poor handling or genetic disposition. They cannot be transmitted to other koi.

### Constipation or Indigestion

A koi that is constipated or suffering from indigestion is often very inactive and usually rests on the bottom of the pond. Its abdomen is generally swollen or bulges. This can be caused by an unbalanced diet, food that doesn't agree with the fish, or overfeeding. You will need to change the food you are feeding the fish. Some experts add 1 teaspoon of Epsom salts for each 5 gallons of water in the hospital tank. Starve the fish for three to five days until it becomes active again. When it resumes normal behavior, feed it live or freeze-dried food for one whole week. After one week, return the fish to the pond. Indigestion and constipation tend to be recurring problems, so make it a point to watch this fish.

## Swim Bladder Disease

Evidenced by an inability to swim properly, swim bladder disease is fairly simple to diagnose. The ailing fish suffers from a loss of balance, swimming on its sides or upside-down or sometimes somersaulting through the water. Swim bladder disease can result from constipation, from bruising of the swim bladder during handling, fighting or breeding, or from bacterial infection associated with poor water quality. These problems have been known to correct themselves as the bruised area heals, but you can't always count on this. If you suspect a bacterial infection, improve water quality and treat the fish with a broad-spectrum antibiotic. If this problem is associated with constipation, your koi is more likely to experience a recurrence. Change your fish's diet and look for improvements.

*If the swim bladder is bruised during handling, swim bladder disease may be a result. This gentleman at a koi show is carefully moving a fish.*

## Tumors

Obvious lumps, bumps or protrusions, tumors occasionally look like a large blister or wart. They have been known to grow to the size of a large screw head. Some tumors can be removed by a veterinarian. Pigmented skin cell tumors are malignant in koi and are characterized by the appearance of multiple tumors

99

on the back. Liver tumors are also commonly found in koi and cause the belly of the fish to be distended. Both types of tumors are untreatable.

## Pop-Eye (Exophthalmus)

This disease causes the eyes to bulge from their sockets and is, therefore, easy to recognize in koi. Fish that develop pop-eye usually do so due to poor water quality and the subsequent chronic stress. Recovery may take several days if efforts are made to improve the water quality. Some feel that food should be withheld for two or three days until pond conditions are corrected.

## INFECTIOUS DISEASES

A disease is considered infectious if it is caused by another organism, such as bacteria, parasites, fungi, viruses and protozoa, and if it can be readily transmitted to other koi.

## BACTERIAL INFECTIONS

### Dropsy or Kidney Bloat

Dropsy is also known as "pinecone" disease because the belly bloats noticeably and the scales stick out, giving

*Isolate any fish that you believe has an infectious disease.*

the fish the appearance of a pinecone. In general, this disease causes the body to swell due to a buildup of fluid in the tissues. Dropsy is caused by the bacteria

*Aeromonas* and *Pseudomonas,* which are associated with water quality problems or low oxygen concentrations. Koi generally don't live more than one week after full-blown dropsy develops. Like constipation and swim bladder disease, fish that survive dropsy tend to have recurring attacks. Because dropsy is contagious, it is best to remove the afflicted fish at once.

Many experts still feel that dropsy is not treatable and that the fish should be immediately removed and painlessly destroyed. Others feel that it can be treated with antibiotic medicated food. Still others suggest creating a special bath by mixing Furanace with water, 250 milligrams to the gallon. This bath should last only one hour and should not be repeated more than three times in three days. It is thought that Furanace can be absorbed by the fish through the skin. If you choose not to use this remedy, you can always try the old-fashioned salt bath described above. If your fish does not respond to treatment in two or three days, it should probably be destroyed.

## Furunculosis (Ulcer Disease)

This bacterial infection will go unnoticed for some time, but then it will spread rapidly. These bacteria infect the flesh under the scales somewhat like skin flukes (see below). However, this infection is first manifested by the appearance of bumps underneath the scales. A short time later, the bumps rupture and create large bleeding ulcers, which is why this ailment is sometimes referred to as "ulcer disease." There is no certain cure for this malady.

While some fish have actually survived, large scars resulting from the infection often prove a problem for them. Fish with these kinds of ulcers should probably be destroyed. The remaining fish should be treated with tetracycline immediately. Some experts argue that all foods should be immediately changed and that any remaining foods be disposed of. Tetracycline treatment can last up to ten days.

## Ulcers (Hole-in-the-Body Disease)

Hole-in-the-body disease is an infection that tends to be internal and that manifests itself in large red ulcers, boils and dark reddening at the bases of the fins. It cannot be mistaken for anchor worms (see below) because anchor-worm ulcers swell up, whereas these tend to eat away into the body.

A salt bath may be too harsh, but the infected fish should be isolated immediately and fed medicated food. At times, antibiotics are required and you will need a veterinarian to prescribe the proper medication. Consult your local koi dealer before proceeding.

## Mouth Fungus (Columnaris Disease)

Mouth fungus is caused by the bacteria *Flexibacter* and manifests itself as a white cottony growth on the mouth. It can also be associated with the gills, back and fins. If left untreated for any length of time, this infection will destroy the entire infected region and lead to eventual death.

Commercial cures are available, but you can begin by isolating the fish and administering the saltwater treatment. Some will start with a salt bath and then use a general bacterial control. Consult with your koi dealer once you have diagnosed the problem.

## Bacterial Fin or Tail Rot

*Your koi should have the full finnage and tails shown here. If fins or tails appear to be missing parts, consult with your koi dealer as to the appropriate treatment.*

Fighting among your fish may result in damage to the fins or tail. The injured area then becomes susceptible to bacterial infection. Fin or tail rot can also be triggered by poor water quality. It is easily detectable, as the fins have missing parts and eventually become shredded. As the disease worsens, the entire fin will be eaten away. There are many broad-spectrum medications that will help you address this problem. Consult your local pet store or koi dealer.

Some experts argue that the best way to treat the infection is by dipping your fish for five minutes in a bath made up of 8 crystals of potassium permanganate to 3 quarts of water. Then, cut off the infected areas of the tail or fin and paint the tail with methylene blue or Mercurochrome. This treatment is rather extreme, and should probably be left to professionals.

## Bacterial Gill Disease

Caused by a number of species of bacteria (most commonly *Myxobacteria*), bacterial gill disease is linked to overcrowding and poor water quality. High water temperatures may accelerate the disease. Symptoms include the destruction and erosion of gill filaments, mucous on the skin and "breathing" behavior at the surface. In some cases, these symptoms can be reversed simply by reducing the koi population in your pond and by improving water quality. Antibacterial treatments may be useful, but the best approach, as always, is to prevent the disease from the start.

## Mycobacteriosis

Mycobacteriosis is caused by the bacteria *Mycobacteria* and causes lesions called granulomas on the internal organs. Because the granulomas are internal and nonspecific, it is difficult to diagnose. Koi with mycobacteriosis develop swollen eyes and distended abdominal regions. Diagnosis can only be confirmed with an internal examination after death. There is no treatment for this disease. If you suspect that one or more of your fish have mycobacteriosis, remove the fish from the pond.

## FUNGAL INFECTIONS

### Fungus

The most common species of fungus infecting tropical fishes is *Saprolegnia*. It is a fuzzy growth that is whiter and easier to notice than velvet. The primary cause of this infection is damage to the mucous layer on the skin, which in turn allows fungal spores to germinate and grow into the skin. Injury, environmental conditions and parasites can damage the protective mucous layer.

Some experts treat this fungal with methylene blue, which they paint on the infected areas. The treated fish is then placed in a ten-day saltwater treatment. Again, commercial remedies are also available.

### Body Slime Fungus

This deadly affliction can kill your fish in two days if not caught in time. The protective mucous coating grows white and starts peeling off as if the fish were shedding its skin. The fins are gradually covered as well. Eventually, the body becomes red with irritation.

Do not hesitate to call your pet store immediately if you see signs of this affliction. Commercial remedies are available, but must be administered quickly. A salt bath with warm temperatures may be a temporary solution, as it should retard growth of the fungus. However, a salt bath will not cure the disease and treatment with a commercial remedy is highly recommended.

*Koi have a protective mucous layer on their skin. Some fungal infections take hold when this mucous layer is damaged.*

## *Branchiomycosis*
This fungal infection attacks the gill of koi causing extreme respiratory stress and gill bleeding. Patches of dead gill tissue are indicative of this disease. Unfortunately, there is no known treatment for this disease and fish succumb quickly within several days. As usual, isolate any fish that you suspect has branchiomycosis.

## VIRAL INFECTIONS
### *Carp Pox*
Carp pox commonly affects koi and its relatives. This is a viral infection that causes a milky white or pinkish-gray waxy film to develop over the fish's skin and fins. The usual pattern of the disease is that it appears, seems to worsen and then disappears.

It is not definitively known what triggers carp pox or how it "runs its cycle." Take the necessary precautions and isolate the infected fish until the film goes away.

This will generally take seven to ten days. High water temperatures often cause the lesions to disappear. Because it does not kill the fish, this ailment is more of an annoyance than a serious problem.

## Spring Viremia of Carp

Characterized by swollen eyes, skin and gill lesions, inability to swim and a swollen abdomen, this highly contagious infection is cause by the virus *Rhabdovirus carpio*. This disease is exacerbated by higher water temperatures and seems to particularly affect young koi. The infection is chronic, meaning that recurrences are common. There is no known treatment and infected fish must be removed from the pond.

## Lymphocystis

Lymphocystis is a common viral disease in fish that is readily diagnosed by the characteristic hard nodules that develop on the body and fins. This chronic condition is not fatal in most cases, but no known treatment exists. Because many of the viral infections are recurring and highly contagious, you should consider the permanent removal of infected fish from your pond.

## PARASITE INFESTATIONS

### Fish Lice

Fish lice are parasitic crustaceans of the species *Argulus* that are very easy to recognize on the surface of your fish. They are round disk-like crustaceans with prominent eyes, sucking disks and a stiletto mouthpart that clamps onto its host refusing to let go. They can move about the host with ease and tend to take on the color of the fish that they parasitize. Often the infected koi will rub up against objects in the tank in an effort to scrape these pests off. Some fish have been known to jump out of the water in an attempt to cleanse themselves of these parasites. These creatures feed by sucking the blood and tissue fluids out of the fish through the skin and scales. Sometimes they occur on the fins, but this is not as satisfying a location for them as on the fish's body. Fish lice can also transmit other microscopic diseases and wounds may develop secondary bacterial infections.

Fortunately, there are a number of high quality commercial products available to control parasites. Your local pet dealer can help you select one. The koi must be quarantined. On larger fish, experts have been known to remove fish lice with forceps or drip hot paraffin wax from a candle onto the parasite. Others recommend giving the afflicted fish a bath for fifteen minutes in a mixture of potassium permanganate and water, which should be extremely light pink. Lice are easily treated, but consult your local pet store or koi dealer for assistance in finding the best treatment.

Most often recommended for treatment for fish lice, anchor worms and leeches are Dipterex, Masoten, Dylox or Nequvon. All bite marks or wounds must be treated on the fish. Dab a little antiseptic Mercurochrome, malachite green or methylene blue on the site. Do not use formalin to kill the parasite, you may also kill your koi because the margin for error is so slim.

*Regularly examine your fish for parasites. Generally, you will be able to see if your koi is carrying external parasites.*

## Anchor Worm

These elongated crustaceans of the genus *Lernaea* also attach to the skin of the fish. Several species of this parasite have been described, but all females have a head with an anchor shape that embeds in the flesh of the host. Your infected koi will rub against anything it can in an attempt to scrape off the parasite. Like fish lice, these creatures cause irritation and localized bleeding at the point of attachment; from this protrudes a white worm that can sometimes grow quite long. Secondary bacterial infection can occur at these points.

Treatment of the anchor worm will include taking the fish out of the water and removing the worm from the aggravated area with a forceps or tweezers. Be sure to carefully follow the instructions accompanying any parasite-control product that you buy.

To remove the worm: Place a wet cloth in your hand. Take hold of the fish in the hand holding the cloth. Make sure to position the fish so that the worm is facing you. With a pair of household tweezers, press as close to the ulcer as possible, but only extract the worm. Make sure not to rip any flesh off the fish and be careful not to break the parasite. This is very dangerous to the fish and you must be extremely cautious when removing a worm in this fashion. It may be best to have an experienced fish keeper do this for you. As in the case with fish lice, be sure to treat the infected area with an antiseptic after removing the parasite. In addition, antibiotic treatment may accelerate the healing of lesions; consult your dealer for a general full-spectrum antibiotic.

## Leeches

Leeches are parasites that may be found on the skin and scales of your koi. These are not the leeches that we see as free-living creatures in lakes and ponds. These are parasitic, worm-like creatures that attach at both ends to your fish, feeding on flesh and blood. They need to be removed as quickly as possible, but not with forceps or tweezers. These parasites are strong and you are likely to do more damage to your koi than to the leeches by trying to pull them off. Call your pet store for advice for commercially produced cures.

Another solution to leeches involves preparing a salt bath with 8 level teaspoons of salt for each gallon of water. Once the salt is sufficiently dissolved, add the koi for no more than ten minutes. The leeches that do not fall off can now be removed with tweezers very easily. Leeches and their eggs may be introduced to your pond by new plants. Consider isolating your new plants in a quarantine tank before introducing them into your pond.

## Flukes—Skin and Gill

As with all infestations, weakened koi will fall victim to flukes before their hardier companions. The gill fluke

*(Dactylogyrus)* is a trematode worm that is very easily detected. It causes the gills to swell up pink and red, and the afflicted fish spends a lot of time near the surface trying to suck in air. Sometimes, a pus-like fluid will be exuded from the gills at this time. These flukes are microscopic parasites that lodge themselves in the gills. Other symptoms include severe color loss, scratching and labored respiration. The skin fluke *(Gyrodactylus)* causes localized swelled areas, excessive mucus and ulcers.

*Parasites are most likely to afflict a weakened fish. A well-maintained pond will go far to keep all of its inhabitants hardy and healthy.*

As with all other parasitic manifestations, the host koi is constantly trying to rub itself against objects to scrape off the infestation. Again, pet stores have pest-control remedies for this flukes, which are quite readily treatable.

Some experts suggest a formaldehyde bath to rid your fish of flukes, but I would only recommend this remedy if commercial solutions are unavailable or are ineffective. Place the koi in a gallon of water. Add 15 drops of formaldehyde every minute for ten minutes. Then remove the koi and place it in a hospital tank. Repeat this process daily for three days. Formaldehyde will kill your fish, so do not haphazardly administer this chemical. Follow the instructions and time it precisely.

## Ich (White Spot)
Raised white spots about the size of salt or granules that appear on the body are the parasite *Ichthyophthirius.* This is one of the most common parasites among

captive fish. It should not be taken lightly, as it will kill your koi if given enough time.

This ailment is so common that there are many commercial ich remedies on the market. Don't be tempted to purchase the least expensive product—consult your dealer and buy the best. Follow standard procedures and remove the fish showing the symptoms and treat it in a quarantine tank.

If an ich treatment is not available to you, give the infected koi in the quarantine tank a ten-day saltwater treatment. It is important to kill this organism before it has an opportunity to infest your entire koi population.

## Velvet

The parasite *Oodinium* causes a golden velvety coat on the body and fins which is referred to as velvet. In orange-colored koi, velvet is sometimes very difficult to detect at first. Commercially produced remedies are best for this parasitic affliction. Some experts use malachite green or the old-fashioned ten-day salt bath. Use the commercial product, but if one is not available, try the salt bath.

## Hole-in-the-Head Disease

Hole-in-the-head disease is caused by the parasite *Hexamita*, an internal parasite. Koi weakened by stress, age or poor water quality are the most susceptible to this parasite. It is characterized by white, stringy feces and enlarged pus-filled sensory pores in the head. Other symptoms include erosion of the skin and muscles that eventually extends to the bones and skull. The lateral line is also a preferred site for these lesions.

On occasion, transferring the koi to a quarantine tank and implementing frequent water changes is enough to cure the fish. Improved nutrition supplemented with vitamin C has been known to improve the condition as well. The prescription drug metronidazole prepared in a bath of 50 mg for every gallon of water is effective at treating this disease. It is recommended that you repeat this treatment after three days.

# SYMPTOMS AND DISEASES AT A GLANCE

| DISEASE | SYMPTOMS |
| --- | --- |
| ANCHOR WORM | A white worm protrudes from a red agitated area on the fish's body. Infested fish rubs against anything it can attempting to scratch off the parasite. |
| BACTERIAL GILL DISEASE | Koi is lethargic, abnormally pale with excess mucous on the skin. Large areas of dead tissue in gills and fish exhibits breathing behavior at surface. |
| BODY SLIME FUNGUS | The protective skin mucous grows white and starts peeling off, as if the fish was shedding or molting. The fins are eventually covered as well. |
| BRANCHIOMYCOSIS | Koi exhibits breathing trouble and patches of dead gill tissue. |
| CARP POX | Whitish or pinkish waxy film develops over koi's skin and fins. |
| CONSTIPATION, INDIGESTION | Koi is very inactive, usually rests on bottom of the pond. Abdominal swelling and bulging is likely to occur. |
| DROPSY (KIDNEY BLOAT) | The abdomen bloats noticeably and the scales stick out like pinecones. |
| FIN OR TAIL ROT | Fins have missing parts; eventually become shredded. Rays become inflamed and entire fin may be eaten away. |
| FISH LICE | Round, disk-shaped, transparent crustaceans that clamp onto host and refuse to let go. Infected koi will rub against objects in an effort to remove the parasites. |
| FUNGUS | Fuzzy growth, whiter in color than velvet. |
| FURUNCULOSIS | Raised bumps under the scales that eventually rupture and cause bleeding ulcers. |
| GILL FLUKES | Gills swell pink and red, fish spends time at the surface gasping for air. Pus-like fluid is exuded from the gills. |

| | |
|---|---|
| HOLE-IN-THE-HEAD | The koi has white stringy feces and enlarged pus-filled sensory pores in the head. Also erosion of the skin and muscles that eventually extends to the bones and skull. |
| ICH | Raised white spots about the size of a salt granule appear on the body and fins. |
| LEECHES | Long, worm-like parasites attached at both ends to the fish that do not come off easily. |
| LYMPHOCYSTIS | Hard nodules on the body and fins of the koi. |
| MOUTH FUNGUS | White cottony growth on mouth sometimes spreading to the gills and other parts. |
| MYCOBACTERIOSIS | Lesions called granulomas on the internal organs of the koi. The fish also develops ulcerations, swollen eyes and a distended abdomen. |
| POP-EYE | Fish's eyes protrude from an inflamed eye socket. |
| SKIN FLUKE | Localized swelled areas, excessive mucous and ulcerations on skin. The fish is constantly trying to rid itself of these parasites by rubbing against objects. |
| SPRING VIREMIA OF CARP | Koi exhibits swollen eyes, lesions of the skin and gills, an inability to swim, a swollen abdomen and is dark in color. |
| SWIM BLADDER DISEASE | Fish swims on its side, upside-down, or somersaults through the water. May be found either on the top or the bottom of the pond. |
| TUMORS | Obvious bumps, lumps, protrusions that sometimes look like a large blister or wart. |
| ULCERS | Large red lesions, boils, dark reddening and bleeding. |
| VELVET | Fuzzy area grows with a yellow or golden color. |

# chapter 9

# Breeding
# Your Koi

Inevitably, as you become more involved in your pond and as you gain experience in the hobby of maintaining a healthy habitat for your fish, you will want to start breeding your koi. The culture of common carp is considered by many to be the oldest form of fish farming in the world, having been practiced in China since 2000 B.C.

Koi breeding is a vast and complex topic, and much has been written about the subject. This relatively brief discussion will address the basics of koi reproduction, spawning behavior and breeding techniques. However, before you set out to seriously breed your koi, I recommend that you consult some of the references listed in chapter 11 for a more complete understanding of this topic.

# Koi Reproduction

Because the reproductive organs of koi, the ovaries and testes, are internal, it is very difficult to sex koi until they reach maturity, which occurs at about 12 inches and 3 years of age. Mature male koi tend to have more slender bodies than the females, and the pectoral fins on males are more pointed and protruding. In breeding season, the males develop several protrusions on the fins and head that resemble spots. The mature females have a thicker, more rounded body shape and they will swell even more in the breeding season when their eggs fully develop.

Koi are considered oviparous or egg-laying fish. The female deposits her eggs in vegetation and the male's sperm fertilizes them externally. The koi egg is smaller than the head of a pin, transparent and adhesive, sticking readily to vegetation. Females may deposit as many as 400,000 eggs during a spawning.

Koi naturally spawn in May and June in temperate regions but continue to spawn year-round in the tropical regions of Indo-Malaysia. Although koi will spawn in water temperatures as low as 63°F, the ideal temperature is 68°F. Spawning is naturally induced by seasonal changes in water temperature, the presence of aquatic plants, fresh

> ## KOI MEETS GIRL
>
> Male koi do not "court" female koi in a way that we would consider to be gentlemanly. During the breeding season, several males will chase, nudge and generally harass a female until she deposits her eggs. The males will then fertilize the eggs. If this event occurs in a well-stocked pond, it is nearly impossible to know which of your koi are the parents of the fry. To diminish "random" breeding, select one female and several of your most attractive male fish for placement in a breeding tank.

oxygen-rich water and the hormonal changes in the male and female. Several males will actively court the female, chasing her and nudging her until she is induced to deposit her eggs in shallow water on living plants. They will then fertilize her eggs by releasing their sperm. Eggs tend to be laid in the early morning hours, and hatching generally occurs within one week at temperatures of 65° to 75°F. Only a very small percentage of eggs and fry will naturally survive in this egg-laying strategy.

# Spawning Koi in Your Pond

If your pond is healthy and your koi are healthy, your fish will spawn when the water temperatures are ideal. In areas of seasonal change, this is usually May or June. As a koi hobbyist, it is up to you to decide whether you want to use the pond for spawning and then collect the eggs for incubation or set up a more controlled environment, such as a spawning tank. If you let nature take its course and allow spawning to naturally occur in your pond, then you will not be able to control bloodlines unless you partition an area of your pond for spawning. In other words, you will not know which fry are the products of which adults if your pond

*The female koi will deposit her eggs on plants in the water. If you want to breed your fish, make sure that your pond is well stocked with plant life.*

contains many kinds of koi. Moreover, eggs deposited by the female will be consumed by the koi if not removed immediately for incubation elsewhere. Within the pond, this problem can be avoided by partitioning the pond with fine mesh and adding a spawning media. You can allow the eggs to hatch in the pond, collect the koi that survive and raise them in a rearing tank. Such partitioning may be logistically difficult depending on your pond design. In these cases, it is best to set up a breeding tank.

## The Breeding Tank

Although koi will naturally spawn in your pond, the serious breeder should set up a breeding or spawning tank. This will allow you to establish special tank conditions that will trigger spawning, it will isolate the parents and the fry so that they can be closely monitored and it will increase the survival of the young fish. In addition, you will be able to control which koi you are going to breed.

The koi breeding tank should be very large, at least 6 to 8 feet in diameter and 3 to 4 feet deep. It should be sturdy but smooth, because koi will often rub up against the sides of the tank. Make sure that adequate aeration is provided. You will also need to add a spawning medium to the tank on which the female can deposit her eggs. A soft or stringy media is preferred, and a mop head, water hyacinths or willow tree branches will do. You can also purchase artificial spawning media. Whatever you choose, make sure that it is free of chemicals and parasites.

## CHOOSING BREEDING STOCK

A very important aspect of koi breeding is the selection of high-quality parent stock. When you breed, you want to produce viable, healthy, colorful offspring, so you must start with excellent parent fish. Those chosen for breeding should be healthy, energetic fish with flawless form, coloration and strong finnage. Some experts recommend that you do not mix major varieties of koi and that you choose fish with snow-

white areas, bright colors and sharply edged patterns. Some well-known breeders will pair one male with one female, but selecting two fish that are at their peak in spawning condition can be difficult. It is recommended that you choose three males and one female for spawning. If the first mating fails, choose other male partners.

*Although it is a logistical challenge, you may try to separate those fish that you want to breed from others in the pond.*

When the time of year is ideal, place the koi you have chosen for spawning in the breeding tank. The water temperature of the breeding tank must be above 75°F during the day. It will naturally cool at night, and this daily change may actually trigger spawning.

Keep a careful eye on these fish, as courtship will become evident within days. The males will begin to bully the female, inducing her to lay her eggs in the

115

spawning media. The tempo of the courtship will increase as the time of egg deposition nears. The eggs are likely to be deposited in the spawning media, but may also be scattered anywhere in the spawning tank.

Spawning and egg-laying generally occur during the early morning hours.

## REMOVE THE PARENTS

Because the parents will consume the eggs, it is critical to remove them. They can either be moved to a rearing tank containing water that is the same high quality and temperature or, quite simply, the parents can be removed and returned to your pond. There will be high mortality in the eggs and fry so don't worry about protecting every egg that is deposited.

*Select energetic, colorful fish of the same variety for breeding purposes.*

## CARING FOR EGGS

The eggs must be kept at a relatively constant temperature with little fluctuation (5° or less), day or night. The eggs will die if the water temperature fluctuates several degrees in a twenty-four-hour period. Within four to seven days, the eggs will begin to hatch, depending on water temperature, which should be between 68° and 75°F. It is not uncommon for fungi to attack your eggs, so you may want to add a weak antifungal agent, such as malachite green, to your tank. A concentration of 0.2mg per liter is recommended.

After hatching, koi fry will instinctively seek protection and hide in the spawning media. They will be able to survive for a few days on the nutrients in their yolk sacs. After that is depleted, they will need to be fed. Koi fry will undergo several changes and larval stages in the first few days as they develop. Every effort must be made to supply large amounts of oxygen to them at this time. Make sure that the water is well aerated. You will know they are ready to feed when they begin to move freely in the mid-water of the tank.

# Feeding Your Koi Fry

The best food for tiny koi is microscopic animals, such as newly hatched brine shrimp. They will also consume very small particles of dried food, such as powdered milk, hard-boiled egg yolk and algae. They will eat continuously, so you will need to feed them throughout the day. As they get larger, increase the size of the food depending on the size of the smallest fish in the tank. In about three to four weeks, your koi will be 0.2 to 0.4 inches in length. If they were hatched in a relatively small incubation tank, they should be moved to a larger pond so as to accelerate their growth.

### BABES IN KOILAND

Koi fry hatch with yolk sacs attached to their bodies. These sacs provide them with nutrition during the first few days of life. After that, you will need to feed the fry with tiny bits of dried food. Baby koi need to be fed very frequently, so if you decide to breed your koi, be prepared to stay home with the offspring.

Be sure to remove uneaten food and other debris from the spawning tank on a continuous basis so that the water does not become fouled. This can be siphoned out as long as you avoid removing the young koi. To control the accumulation of ammonia and nitrites, you should also add fresh water to the tank on a continuous basis. If you are adding tap water, make sure that it is has been aerated to allow chlorine to evaporate. Don't hesitate to use your pH and other test kits to monitor the water quality in your incubation (rearing) tank.

## Culling

Your koi fry will grow rapidly and you can easily end up with several thousand fish from a spawn. Within the first month, you should begin to cull your offspring. This will reduce your number of koi to manageable levels while allowing you to select the highest quality koi. Professional breeders usually cull about 90 percent of the fry. The first step is to remove deformed or weak fish from the brood. Then, as you progressively cull, select for color and markings, leaving only the best specimens.

The first several months of raising your koi will be committed to intensively feeding and culling until you are left with high quality offspring of several inches in length. Much of the decision-making in culling will depend on your personal tastes about the color, shape and size of your fish. Be sure to increase the size of the tank that houses your koi as they get larger. Juvenile fish a few inches in length can be added to your main pond, but this will make culling very difficult.

*Professional breeders who will show their fish often cull up to 90 percent of the fry. Their goal is to raise only the highest quality koi.*

As your koi get larger, they will require less food. At 1 month of age, koi need about 5 percent of their body weight in food and should be fed little and often. As they get older, decrease this to about 2 percent of their body weight. Be sure to choose food that is appropriately sized for the smallest individuals in the tank. You will notice that the koi that grow most quickly tend to be less attractive and resemble the common carp in appearance. This is because the prettier koi are highly inbred and not as hardy as the wild carp.

part four

# Beyond
## the •
# Basics

# chapter 10

# Glossary
## of Japanese
# Koi Terms

*Ai:* blue

*Aka:* red/orange

*Akame:* eye with a red iris

*Akebi:* light blue

*Asagi:* blue

*Atama:* head

*Atama Ga Hageru:* clearness of the head

*Bai:* plum

*Bekko:* tortoiseshell pattern

*Beni:* orange base

*Beta-Gin:* uneven scales

*Boke:* faded color

*Botan:* rose

*Bozu:* bald head

*Bu:* size

*Budo:* grape

*Bunka:* shiny pectoral fins

*Cha:* brown

*Chupa:* medium-quality koi

*Dagoi:* poor-quality koi

*Danmoro:* koi with step pattern

*Doitsu:* German

*Enazuma:* lightning-shaped red pattern from head to tail

*Fuji Sanke:* metallic luster on the head

*Gaku:* deformed koi

*Gin:* silver

*Gin Kabuto:* silver helmet

*Go:* five

*Goior Koi:* wild carp

*Goke:* scale of a fish

*Goromo:* robed, blue-black or purple overlay

*Goshiki:* five colors

*Goten Zakura:* bunch of grapes pattern

*Hachi:* head

*Hachiware:* black line design across head

*Hachizumi:* black lightning pattern across head

*Hajiro:* white tips on pectoral fins

*Haku:* white

*Hana:* flowery

*Hanatsuki:* red marking that reaches the mouth

*Hanazumi:* black spot pattern around nose and mouth

*Hariwaki:* white metallic with a gold pattern

*Hi:* red

*Hiban:* red pattern

*Higoi:* rouge

*Hikari:* metallic or shiny

*Hisoku:* yellow-green coloration

*Hoo Aka:* red gill plates

*Hookazuki:* red cheeks

*Iarisumi:* small black spots

*Ike:* pond

*Inazuma:* lightning pattern

*Ippon Moyo:* solid red from head to tail

*Iro:* color

*Jihada:* skin texture

*Jiro:* white

*Kabuto:* helmet

*Kagami:* mirror

*Kaku:* square or rectangle

*Kana:* male koi

*Kanoko:* dappled

*Karasu:* black koi

*Kasane:* black on red

*Kata Moyo:* pattern on the koi's side

*Kawa:* no scales

*Kawari:* nonmetallic

*Kesuki:* uneven color pattern

*Ki:* yellow

*Kin:* gold

*Kin Kabuto:* golden helmet

*Koborehi:* scattered red

*Koboresumi:* scattered black

*Koi:* carp

*Koke:* scale

*Komoyo:* small pattern

*Konjo:* very dark

*Koromo:* robed

*Koshi:* green

*Kozumi:* small black spots

*Kuchi:* mouth

*Kuchibeni:* red lips

*Kujaku:* peacock

*Kuro:* black

*Ma:* wild

*Magoi:* wild carp

*Makibara:* red marking that wraps around lower part of body

*Makigari:* black pattern extending from abdomen to upper body

*Makikomi:* pattern extending from upper body to abdomen

*Matsuba:* pinecone

*Men:* face

*Mena:* female

*Menkaburi:* red head

*Midori:* green

*Mizu:* very light blue

*Momiji:* autumn colors—red, purple, white

*Moyo:* patterned

*Moyomono:* one pattern

*Muji:* nothing else—solid color

*Mujimono:* one metallic color

*Munabire:* pectoral fin

*Naruni:* light blue pattern

*Nezu:* gray or tarnished silver

*Ni:* two

*Nidan:* two red patterns on a white body

*Nosezumi:* black pattern overlapping red pattern

*Obire:* tail fin

*Odome:* the area between the last pattern and the anal fin

*Ogon:* one color koi

*Omoyo:* single large wavy pattern covering back

*Orenji:* orange

*Parrachina* or *Platena:* white metallic, platinum

*Pongoi:* high-quality koi

*Rin:* scales

*Sakura:* cherry blossom

*San:* three

*Sandan:* three patches of red

*Sanke:* three colors

*Sanshoku:* three colors

*Sarasa:* red spots on back

*Sebire:* dorsal fin

*Shageru:* to perfect

*Shashikome:* scales covering the edge of the pattern

*Shikaku:* head pattern is square or rectangular

*Shiku:* colored

*Shimekai:* to stunt growth for color intensity

*Shimi:* small black spots

*Shinzo:* heart-shaped

*Shiro:* white

*Shiro Matsuba:* white body with black pinecone pattern

*Shitsu:* quality

*Showa:* 1926 to 1989 koi era

*Shusui:* autumn water

*Sokozumi:* barely visible black shadowing

*Sui:* water

*Sumi:* black, black patches

*Sumi Nagashi:* black with scales outlined in white

*Sure:* external injury

*Taike:* body conformation

*Taisho:* 1912 to 1926 koi era

*Tama Gin:* pearl scale

*Tancho:* red spot on head

*Tatigoi:* small, high-quality koi

*Tebire:* pectoral fin

*Teri:* gloss

*Tobi:* cannibalistic fry

*Tobihi:* splattered red markings

*Tora:* tiger

*Tosai:* first year

*Tsubo:* black patterns on white skin

*Tsubozumi:* black spots on white area

*Tsubu Gin:* pearl scales

*Uroko:* scales

*Utsuri:* reflection

*Utsurimono:* black base with one color

*Yamabuki:* pale yellow (flower)

*Yodan:* four patch pattern

*Yogyo:* young fish, fish farming

*Yon:* four

*Yoroi:* armor

*Zuiun:* light purple

*Zuninaburi:* red forehead

# chapter 11

# Resources

There are an amazing number of resources available to the koi enthusiast. Koi exhibitions, Koi societies, Internet resources, books, and magazines delve into the many aspects of koi-keeping. This book provides the basics, and readers are encouraged to take advantage of these resources as their interest in koi explodes.

## Exhibitions

Koi have been exhibited in Japan for years, and the popularity of these shows is spreading rapidly throughout the world. At exhibitions, koi are professionally judged based on several criteria relative to shape, color and patterns. The Japanese have established a hierarchy of form, color and pattern that determines the desirability and value of a particular koi. Shows range from very small to very large and prizes vary from moderate to substantial. A prize-winning koi is very valuable if its owner desires to sell it.

Most exhibitions and competitions are organized by regional koi societies that have been established around the world. Koi are generally displayed in blue plastic pools that are 6 to 10 feet in diameter.

The koi are classified by size (ranging from 6 to 22 inches), colors and patterns.

As your interest in koi develops and you master the essentials to keeping happy healthy koi, your interest in showing off your fish may develop as well. The best way to become involved in exhibitions is to join and become active in one of the hundreds of koi societies.

# Koi Societies

The popularity of koi-keeping as a hobby has caused an incredible cohesion of hobbyists into koi clubs and societies. At least thirty-six states in the United States have regional koi clubs that unite the common interests of koi-keepers, sponsor koi exhibitions and provide an invaluable source of new information about koi. If you are serious about keeping koi, then I strongly recommend that you join one of these societies. A good way to find the closest koi club in your area is to contact the Associated Koi Clubs of America (AKCA).

# Internet Resources

A simple search engine on the Internet will generate over 600,000 hits when you query it with the word koi. Granted, not all of these hits are valid koi Web sites but you can be sure that there is no lack of koi-related information on the Internet. The AKCA has a Web page that not only lists its affiliated clubs in the United States but also the latest books, magazines, exhibitions and general koi information. Their Internet address is www.koiusa.com. Most of the major koi distributors and dealers have Internet sites as well, placing the purchase of koi and koi supplies at your fingertips. If you have Internet access, then you have access to a wealth of information about koi. However, as with all Internet resources, be aware that the presence of a Web site does not guarantee that the information it provides is valid. Surf carefully!

# Magazines

There are several magazines dedicated to the avocation of keeping koi. Timely articles will give you the latest in koi biology, feeding, husbandry, breeding, exhibition and the many other topics associated with this popular fish. These include:

*Koi USA*
P.O. Box 1
Midway City, CA 92655

*Mid-Atlantic Koi*
3290 Shaker Ct.
Montclair, NJ 22026

*PONDKEEPER* Magazine
Garden Pond Promotions, Inc.
1000 Whitetail Ct.
Duncansville, PA 16635

# Books

There are literally hundreds of books written about the many aspects of koi. For decades, koi have been revered for their beauty and elegance and have thus motivated many to write about this magnificent fish. Your local library, on-line bookstores, local bookstores and koi clubs provide access to books dedicated to koi and koi ponds. Recommended titles include:

Barrie, A. *The Professional's Book of Koi*. Neptune, NJ: Tfh Publications, Inc., 1992.

Blasiola, G. *Koi*. Hauppauge, NY: Barron's Educational Series, Inc., 1995.

Conrad, R. *An Owner's Guide to the Garden Pond*. New York: Howell Book House, 1998.

Rothbard, S. *Koi Breeding*. Neptune, NJ: Tfh Publications, Inc., 1997.

Stoskopf, M. *Fish Medicine*. Philadelphia, PA: W. B. Saunders Co., 1993.

Waddington, P. *Koi Kichi*. Cheshire, England: Peter Waddington Ltd., 1997.

Wisner, S.C. and F. A. Simon. *Keeping Koi*. New York: Sterling Publishing Co., Inc., 1996.